ALBERT KESSELRING

LEADERSHIP ■ STRATEGY ■ CONFLICT

PIER PAOLO BATTISTELLI ■ ILLUSTRATED BY ADAM HOOK

First published in 2012 by Osprey Publishing
Midland House, West Way, Botley, Oxford OX2 0PH, UK
44-02 23rd St, Suite 219, Long Island City, NY 11101, USA
E-mail: info@ospreypublishing.com

Print ISBN: 978 1 84908 735 3
PDF e-book ISBN: 978 1 84908 736 0
EPUB e-book ISBN: 978 1 78096 883 4

Editorial by Ilios Publishing Ltd, Oxford, UK (www.iliospublishing.com)
Page layout by The Black Spot
Index by Mike Parkin
Typeset in Stone Serif and Officina Sans
Maps by Mapping Specialists Ltd
Originated by PDQ Digital Media Solutions Ltd, Suffolk
Printed in China through Worldprint Ltd.

12 13 14 15 16   10 9 8 7 6 5 4 3 2 1

A CIP catalogue record for this book is available from the British Library.

www.ospreypublishing.com

Acknowledgements

The author wishes to thank the following for their help and support: Count Ernesto G. Vitetti, Professor Piero Crociani, Dottor Andrea Molinari, Tenente Colonnello Filippo Cappellano.

Artist's note

Readers may care to note that the original paintings from which the colour plates in this book were prepared are available for private sale. All reproduction copyright whatsoever is retained by the Publishers. All enquiries should be addressed to:

Scorpio Gallery, PO Box 475, Hailsham, East Sussex, BN27 2SL, UK

The Publishers regret that they can enter into no correspondence upon this matter.

Front-cover image
© CORBIS

The Woodland Trust

Osprey Publishing are supporting the Woodland Trust, the UK's leading woodland conservation charity, by funding the dedication of trees. Command Series Albert Kesselring

TABLE OF RANKS

German	British	USA
Leutnant	Second Lieutenant	Second Lieutenant
Oberleutnant	Lieutenant	First Lieutenant
Hauptmann	Captain	Captain
Major	Major	Major
Oberstleutnant	Lieutenant-Colonel	Lieutenant-Colonel
Oberst	Colonel	Colonel
Brigadier	*	
Generalmajor	Brigadier-General	
Generalleutnant	Major-General	Major-General
General der… **	Lieutenant-General	Lieutenant-General
Generaloberst	General	General
Generalfeldmarschall	Field Marshal	General of the Army

Notes:
* equivalent to *Generalmajor* and brigadier-general but not a general officer
** rank completed with the arm of service or speciality of the owner (e.g. Rommel was a *General der Panzertruppen*)

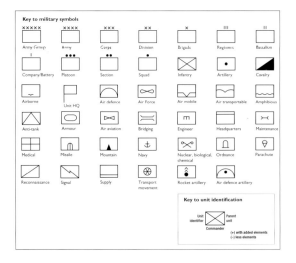

CONTENTS

INTRODUCTION

Albert Kesselring's name will forever be linked to the Italian campaign of World War II, from the epic battles of 1943–44, such as Salerno, Cassino and Anzio, to the mass killing of 335 Italians in reprisal for a partisan attack in Rome of March 1944. But Kesselring's career amounted to much more, even though it is perhaps less well known than that of other German generals such as Rommel, Guderian or Manstein.

Kesselring served with distinction in World War I, and became a staff officer in 1917, despite not attending the Kriegsakademie. In 1940, at the age of 55, he was appointed *Generalfeldmarschall*, jumping one rank and becoming one of only five Luftwaffe generals to reach that rank (one of them, Robert von Greim, was only promoted on 25 April 1945). He was the 14th soldier of the German armed forces to be awarded the coveted Diamonds to the Oakleaves and Swords to his Knight's Cross, and one of just 12 Luftwaffe officers to receive this award (and the only one, along with General Bernhard Ramcke, who was not a pilot). Although not as famous as other German generals or Luftwaffe officers, Kesselring was easily recognizable: a tall, solid man, with an easy smile that earned him the nickname 'Smiling Albert'. As a commander, he had a reputation as a paternal figure. And yet Kesselring is not one of those German generals who earned their fame, either as a theorist of warfare or as a field commander, during the early years of the blitzkrieg, the lightning war. As chief of staff of the newly created Luftwaffe, Kesselring's legacy was to cancel once and for all the project of the long-range, strategic bomber, which the Luftwaffe was unable to develop during the war. The success of his Luftflotte 2 in Holland and Belgium during the early stage of the campaign in the West in May 1940 was soon tarnished by failures, first at Dunkirk and then in the Battle of Britain a few months later. Appointed Oberbefehlshaber Süd (Commander-in-Chief South) in December 1941 with the task of overseeing the air and naval war in the Mediterranean, Kesselring temporarily restored the broken supply link with North Africa, but was eventually unable to maintain it satisfactorily. When finally forced to decide between attacking Malta or Egypt, the Führer acted on Rommel's advice and chose Egypt, despite Kesselring's objections. Five months later, Kesselring took no pleasure in Rommel's defeat in North Africa, which was partly a result of the logistical difficulties that he had predicted. It was left to Kesselring to save the day, and what was left of the Axis forces in the area, by establishing the Tunisian bridgehead. Less than a year later, Kesselring won a last struggle with Rommel when Hitler gave him command of the German forces in Italy, a decision that had a profound effect on both his military career, as well as his life.

By then, Kesselring had a reputation as a general and a commander who could be relied upon in a time of crisis, the man able to ensure small 'miracles' that prevented the enemy from exploiting surprise attacks or from breaking through the German lines; the one who managed to restore the situation against all odds. Not surprisingly, when he was appointed Oberbefehlshaber West (Commander-in-Chief West) in March 1945, replacing Rundstedt after the bridge at Remagen fell into American hands, he introduced himself to his staff with the words 'I'm the new wonder weapon'. Obviously, not even he

Albert Kesselring at the peak of his career, sporting at his neck the Knight's Cross with Oakleaves, Swords and Diamonds (the highest German decoration) awarded him on 19 July 1944. (Count Ernesto G. Vitetti)

could work the miracle of changing the fortunes of a war already lost, something Kesselring was perfectly aware of even before surrendering to the Allies two months later. But unlike the old soldiers who never die, Kesselring was not going to simply fade away. A year after he had been a major witness at the Nuremberg trial, Kesselring was himself put on trial for the reprisals in Rome in March 1944. He was not the only German general to suffer such a fate, either among those who served in the Italian campaign or simply among those who fought during World War II, but unlike many other trials this one was to achieve widespread notoriety.

The vociferous debate that followed Kesselring's sentence of death not only led to it being commuted and then suspended, but was also closely related to the wider issue of the German rehabilitation. Kesselring's fate still fascinates historians, and proves that his story and character were more complex than they have often been given credit for.

EARLY YEARS

Albert Konrad Kesselring was born on 30 November 1885 in Marktsteft, near Würzburg in Bavaria. His father, Carl Adolf, was a primary school teacher who had married his second cousin, Rosina Kesselring. As Albert later remarked, there was absolutely no tradition of military service in the family, although thanks to his mother's family (who owned a brewery), he could enjoy a certain social status. The Kesselring family moved at first to Wunsiedel, then to Bayreuth, where they settled in 1898. There Albert

Kesselring took his *Abitur*, the classical grammar school degree, in 1904 with a dissertation in which he emphasized the ties of his nationalistic feelings toward Germany with his Bavarian patriotism. His teachers describe a good, frank boy, who was sometimes too serious (apparently, he seldom smiled, in contrast to the future 'smiling Albert' image). They regarded him as only moderately talented, uncertain in his judgement, cumbersome in his thinking and therefore prone to becoming confused and upset. He excelled in gymnastics, drawing, religion, languages (German and French), mathematics, physics and history, while Greek and Latin were only average. In spite of his shortcomings, Kesselring succeeded by working furiously hard when the occasion demanded. This quality certainly helped when the young Kesselring decided to pursue a career as a soldier.

Despite the lack of a military background, he joined the army as a volunteer aspirant officer (*Fahnenjunker*) on 20 July 1904, a remarkable achievement considering that requirements for officer candidates were actually higher in Bavaria than in Prussia, with less than ten per cent of candidates coming from teachers' families, as opposed to 80 per cent who were from the upper classes. The choice of unit, 2. Bayerische Fussartillerie Regiment (2nd Bavarian Foot Artillery Regiment), stationed at Metz, then part of Germany, was a kind of compromise; Kesselring did not like walking, which excluded the infantry, and could not afford to join the cavalry, the elite of the German Army. Following the German practice for officer candidates, Kesselring was promoted first to *Unteroffizier* on 25 October 1904, then *Fähnrich* (officer candidate) on 4 February 1905, and, following the customary period spent at the Kriegsschule in Munich between 1 March 1905 and 25 January 1906 (one of the ten military academies established in Germany to guarantee a uniform training for all officers) Albert Kesselring was commissioned *Leutnant* on 8 March 1906.

Service in the army revealed Kesselring's best qualities; from 1 October 1908 to 18 March 1910 he attended the Artillerie und Ingenieurschule (the Artillery and Engineers' School) at Munich and, between 4 and 22 June 1912, he underwent training as a balloon observer at the Luftschiffabteilung, the Air Balloon Battalion. Comments about the young officer were more than favourable: in January 1909 his regimental commander remarked that he was one of the best, with a promising career ahead of him. He exercised great influence and authority on his subordinates, who he trained with skill, calm and excellent results. His interest in technical matters advanced and, on 1 October 1912, Kesselring became adjutant of the first battalion of the Fussartillerie Regiment, and was promoted *Oberleutnant* on 25 October 1913. Yet although he was marked out as one of the 20 officers selected every year to attend the Bavarian Kriegsakademie (the war school), he somehow failed to apply, temporarily losing the chance of becoming a general staff officer, the basic step for a career in the German Army. This is one of the big question marks over Kesselring's early years, the other one being his marriage to Pauline Anna Keyssler on 29 March 1910. It seems to have been an arranged marriage, made slightly awkward by the presence of his mother-in-law, who initially lived with the young couple. They had no children of their own and in 1913 adopted Rainer, the young son of Albert's second cousin.

The outbreak of World War I saw Kesselring still in Metz, at first engaged in the aborted attempt to break through the French defences at Nancy and, from November 1914, in Flanders. On 5 December, he was transferred to the headquarters of 1. Königlich Bayerischen Füssartillerie Brigade (Royal Bavarian Foot Artillery Brigade), where he served at first as adjutant and then (from 13 March 1915) as officer with special duties, before being back as adjutant with the second battalion of the Fussartillerie Regiment between 8 May and 2 September 1915. Kesselring was transferred to the HQ of the Fussartillerie Brigade on 3 September 1915 and, promoted *Hauptmann* on 19 May 1916. On 6 March 1917 he became adjutant at the Königlich Bayerischen Artillerie Kommandeur 3 (Royal Bavarian Artillery Command). Shortly after he took the position, on 9 April 1917 the British attack at Vimy Ridge tore a 12km (7-mile) gap in the German lines. On 11 April Kesselring was at the front and helped to restore the situation, thus preventing a German collapse. This earned him enthusiastic reports and eventually (after a course at the army gas protection school at Berlin on 8–13 October), on 24 November 1917, a transfer to the Eastern Front, to the staff of the 2. Königlich Bayerischen Landwehr Division (Royal Bavarian Territorial Division) as a general staff candidate.

This filled a noticeable gap in Kesselring's career, and on 4 January 1918 he returned to the Western Front as a general staff officer, first with the staff of Armeeoberkommando 6 (Sixth Army) then, from 15 April, with the staff of III Königlichen Bayerischen Armee Korps (Royal Bavarian Army Corps). Although Kesselring did not serve in the trenches or even at the front line, he was awarded the Iron Cross first and second class, and his reputation won him a place in the 100,000-man Reichswehr after the war, despite some acid criticism concerning the high opinion he had of himself and his lack of understanding of the difficulties of the frontline soldiers.

Temporarily barred from staff duties because of an ill-advised dispute with the *Freikorps* and social democrats during demobilization, Kesselring was a battery commander from 24 August 1919, at first with Artillerie-Regiment 24, then from 1 January 1921 with Artillerie-Regiment 7. On 1 October 1922 he was assigned to the Reichswehr Ministerium (the Reich Defence Ministry) in Berlin, being eventually transferred to the Truppenamt (Troop Office) on 1 April 1924, where he held several positions under leading personalities such as Seeckt and Blomberg. Promoted *Major* on 1 April 1925, from 1 April 1929 he had a one-year tour of duty with the troops that earned him promotion to *Oberstleutnant* on 1 February 1930. On 5 May 1930 Kesselring was back to the Reichswehr Ministerium, eventually becoming commanding officer of III/Artillerie-Regiment 4 on 1 February 1932. On 1 October of the

Kesselring with Erhard Milch (the powerful secretary of state for air) during field exercises held in Germany, 1937. The relationship between the two was never easy and eventually Kesselring abandoned the position of Chief of Staff of the Luftwaffe because of him. (Count Ernesto G. Vitetti)

same year he was promoted *Oberst,* reaching the peak of his career in the army, before transferring (unofficially) to the Luftwaffe on 1 October 1933.

MILITARY LIFE

In his memoirs, Kesselring suggests that he was slightly reluctant to transfer to the nascent Luftwaffe, but while career progression in the Reichswehr was excruciatingly slow, service in the new branch offered unparalleled possibilities. Furthermore, it was actually Blomberg who personally selected high profile individuals for key positions in the Luftwaffe, which should have included people like Manstein and Halder, the future Army Chief of Staff. The choice of Kesselring was particularly apt given his technical background and his skills as a staff officer, and it did not take long before rewards started to come his way.

Kesselring was officially dismissed from the army and, as a civilian, was transferred to the Reichs Luftfahrt Ministerium (RLM, the Reich Air Ministry) on 1 October 1933, just six months after it was formed and nine months after Hitler's rise to power in Germany. Appointed chief of the administrative office, Kesselring worked very closely with the renowned first chief of air staff (the Luftkommandoamt, or Air Headquarters Office), General Walther Wever, the powerful state secretary of the air ministry Erhard Milch and the minister himself, Hermann Göring. Given the provisional rank of *Kommodore*, at the age of 48 Kesselring learned to fly, and was promoted *Generalmajor* on 1 April 1934. Following the official creation of the Luftwaffe on 26 February 1935, Kesselring became *Generalleutnant* on 1 April 1936 – demonstrating a far faster career progression than he could ever have hoped for in the army. On 3 June 1936 Wever was killed in an air accident, and on 12 June Kesselring was chosen to be the new chief of the Luftkommandoamt.

Göring examines the situation, leaning over opeational maps during the Battle of Britain. To his right (wearing the overcoat) is Kesselring, who is talking to another officer. (Count Ernesto G. Vitetti)

Whatever hopes he may have had in this phase of his new career, it was soon crushed by the reality of power struggles and personality clashes within the air ministry. Wever's greatest achievement was his ability to work with all the key high profile personalities and to run things smoothly, which was certainly not Kesselring's style. Rivalries and power struggles between Kesselring and Milch increased, and eventually Kesselring asked to be dismissed from his position. This particular event was also related to a turning point in the development of the Luftwaffe for, on 1 June 1937, the Luftkommandoamt was reorganized and became the Generalstab der Luftwaffe (General Staff of the Luftwaffe). It is also interesting to see how Kesselring's position proved hard to fill: his successor, Hans-Jürgen Stumpff, held the positions for less than two years, only to be replaced by Hans Jeschonnek in

German paratroopers in Holland, May 1940. Although it eventually forced the Dutch surrender, the air operation of May 1940 was not fully successful mostly because of Hitler's and Göring's interference with the plans. (*Signal*)

February 1939. The fact that he committed suicide in August 1943 gives some idea of the stresss of the position of chief of staff. On 1 June 1937 Kesselring was promoted *General der Flieger* and was appointed commander of Luftkreis III, the Luftwaffe area command for the Dresden zone. From 4 February 1938 he was commander of Luftwaffe Gruppenkommando 1 in north-eastern Germany (Berlin) which, following mobilization on 1 September 1939 when the war with Poland broke out, became Luftflotte 1.

Kesselring led Luftflotte 1 in the war against Poland and on 30 September 1939 was awarded the Knight's Cross by Hitler himself. Yet another accident was to drive Kesselring's career away from established paths. On 10 January 1940 a German plane landed by mistake in Belgium, and the staff officer on board was captured, along with all his papers, which related to the planned

As Oberbefehlshaber Süd Kesselring also had to deal with the Kriegsmarine in the Mediterranean; to his right is Vize-Admiral Eberhard Weichold, the commander of Deutsche Marinekommando Italien (German Naval Command, Italy) until March 1943. (Count Ernesto G. Vitetti)

A Messerschmitt Bf 109 pilot prepares to fly, September 1939. The Polish Air Force was not destroyed on the ground in the first days of war, but fought valiantly until being overwhelmed by mid-September. (*Signal*)

attack against Belgium and the north of France. The so-called 'Mechelen Incident' put an end to the career of General Felmy and, following his dismissal from the position of commander of Luftflotte 2, Kesselring replaced him on 12 January 1940. This was the key that opened the door to the last phase of Kesselring's career. As commander of Luftflotte 2 he was put in charge of the northern shoulder of the attack on the West that started on 10 May 1940. Notably, he was directly responsible for airborne operations against the Netherlands and for protecting the push into Belgium down to the Channel. Holland's surrender followed immediately after the bombing of Rotterdam on 14 May, and on the 20th, Panzer divisions were on the Channel coast, closing the trap around British and French forces. With the fall of Boulogne on 25 May, followed the next day by the fall of Calais, Kesselring's air forces were heavily engaged for the first time against the RAF in the battle for Dunkirk. This ended on 5 June, when the German forces started the second phase of the campaign, attacking central France, and forcing the French surrender on 22 June.

Following the victory in the West on 19 July 1940, Hitler promoted 11 generals to the rank of *Generalfeldmarschall*, one of whom was Kesselring (who skipped the rank of *Generaloberst*). Still in command of Luftflotte 2, he was directly engaged in the air war against Britain, along with Generalfeldmarschall Hugo Sperrle (commander of Luftflotte 3), during the summer and the autumn of 1940. The first phase, lasting from 10 July to 7 August, was aimed at coastal convoys and harbours; the second phase started on 8 August with attacks against targets in southern England, even though *Adlertag* (Eagle Day), the official start of the German air offensive, was on 13 August. Until 23 August the Luftwaffe carried out heavy attacks against airfields and other targets in southern England, and on 24 August a new phase began, with increased attacks extending to the London area. From 7 September the Luftwaffe focused mainly on bombing London, which reached its peak on 15 September, eventually lasting until the end of the month when the Luftwaffe was forced to acknowledge defeat. In November tactics were altered slightly and the Blitz began. The Luftwaffe carried out night after night of debilitating raids until May 1941, when Luftflotte 2 left France for the east. On 22 June Germany attacked the Soviet Union in Operation *Barbarossa*, and Kesselring's forces were sent to support the land operations, with Heeresgruppe Mitte.

In January 1941 the Luftwaffe spearheaded the arrival of the German forces in the Mediterranean and in North Africa, but during the summer British air and naval intervention from Malta threatened German supply convoys from Italy to Libya. In September Jeschonnek, the Chief of the Air Staff, suggested that Kesselring should be transferred to the Mediterranean, and after a direct order from Hitler in October, Kesselring moved on, while Luftflotte 2 was still fully engaged in support of the attack on Moscow. On 28 November 1941 Kesselring arrived in Rome, followed shortly by the HQ of the Luftflotte 2 and the bulk of II Flieger Korps, just before the Soviet counterattack on the Eastern Front put an end to the invincibility of the Wehrmacht. On 2 December 1941 Kesselring was also appointed Oberbefehlshaber Süd (OB Süd, Commander-in-Chief South), responsible for the air war in the Mediterranean and North Africa, and bound to close co-operation with other forces. On 25 February 1942 Kesselring was awarded the Oak Leaves to his Knight's Cross, followed on 18 July by the Swords. Heavy air raids against Malta restored the flow of supplies for North Africa, but Kesselring

realized the supply situation could only be solved by seizing the island and therefore supported the Italian plan to assault it. Rommel's victory in the Western Desert in May–June 1942 eventually led to the cancellation of the plan, with the result that the supply situation was critical again after Rommel's failure to break through at El Alamein.

In September 1942 Hitler considered Kesselring as a possible replacement for Generalfeldmarschall Wilhelm Keitel at the head of the Oberkommando der Wehrmacht, but the worsening situation in the Mediterranean prevented any change. On 4 November 1942 Rommel's forces began their withdrawal from Egypt, and on the 8th the Allies landed in French North Africa; Kesselring reacted swiftly and quickly established a bridgehead at Tunis that enabled the Axis forces to maintain a North African stronghold until the final surrender on 13 May 1943. Six weeks later, on 26 June, Kesselring relinquished command of Luftflotte 2 to Wolfram von Richthofen while

Junkers Ju 87 Stuka dive bombers just transferred to Sicily from the Eastern Front, as shown by the yellow markings that were commonly used in the East (white was the colour for the Mediterranean). (*Signal*)

Colleagues, rivals, commanders – but never friends. Kesselring confronts Rommel face-to-face in North Africa during one of his many inspection trips. (Count Ernesto G. Vitetti)

A German machine-gun nest in Italy. Even though the Italian campaign is considered a masterpiece of strategy, it was in fact only successful when the Germans fought in defence, since both the counterattacks at Salerno and at Anzio ended in failure. (Author's collection)

retaining his duties as OB Süd (as sanctioned by Hitler's directive of 28 January 1943). He was now in charge of coordinating all Reich forces in the area, under direct orders from Hitler. The nominal Italian command ended shortly after the Allied landing in Sicily on 10 July 1943, with the German commanders taking over by mid-July to early August. Following Mussolini's downfall on 25 July, Hitler sent more German forces to northern Italy under Rommel's command, and from 22 August Kesselring was *de facto* acting army group commander following the arrival of General Heinrich von Vietinghoff's AOK 10 in southern Italy. Kesselring was shocked by the Italian surrender, as he was convinced that the Italians would fight against the Allied invasion of their mainland. The Allied landing at Salerno on 8 September 1943 began the Italian campaign and the last phase of Kesselring's career.

On 15 August, Rommel assumed command of Heeresgruppe B in northern Italy, and a boundary line was established some 50km (30 miles) south of Florence between his and Kesselring's commands. From 8 September German forces in Italy were busy disarming the Italians and, under Kesselring's command, fighting the Allied landing at Salerno. The German counterattack against the beachhead started on 13–14 September and seriously threatened the Allied forces until reinforcements arrived and the British Eighth Army approached from the south. Kesselring was forced to call the attacks back on 18 September. What followed was a staged withdrawal aimed at gaining time and wearing the Allied forces down, while completing a defensive line running across Italy, a successful tactic that favourably impressed Hitler. Having initially selected Rommel to take over overall command in Italy on 17 October, on 5 November Hitler decided to appoint Kesselring theatre commander with effect from the 21st. Kesselring became Oberbefehlshaber Südwest (Commander-in-Chief South-west) and Commander-in-Chief of Heeresgruppe C.

On 20 October the US Fifth Army started the last phase of the offensive that, by December, was to reach the positions of the Gustav Line at Monte Cassino, where fierce battles were fought until May 1944 and the Allies would see their efforts to break through the line repeatedly frustrated. In an attempt to solve the stalemate, on 22 January 1944 the US VI Corps landed just south of Rome, at Anzio, which presented Kesselring with one of the most critical situations of the entire campaign. His swift reaction eventually prevented an Allied breakout from the beachhead, but once again the counterattack ended in a failure and the Anzio bulge turned into a serious threat when the Allied forces started their offensive in May.

It was mostly because of General Clark's desire to be first into Rome in May–June 1944 that a large portion of German forces escaped encirclement, but not even the mistakes of Allied commanders or the Normandy landings could change the dramatic situation faced by Kesselring in Italy. By the end of July 1944 the Allied forces had almost reached the Gothic Line after an advance of some 300km (186 miles) in about two months. The award of the Diamonds to the Oakleaves and Swords to the Knight's Cross on 19 July was hardly of help to Kesselring, who faced the fact that the northern Apennine defence line was not yet ready. From 25 August the Gothic Line was attacked by the Eighth Army, which soon threatened to break through the German defences; this was the start of a long-lasting offensive that only came to end in December 1944, after months of bitter fighting and frustration for the Allies, who were greatly hampered by terrain and weather. Kesselring did not fight the whole battle, for on 23 October his car collided with a towed gun and he was severely wounded with a skull fracture. He was hospitalized, but was back on duty on 15 January 1945 and soon given a new assignment: on 9 March he replaced the disgraced Rundstedt as Oberbefehlshaber West (Commander-in-Chief West). On 28 April 1945 Kesselring became again Oberbefehlshaber Süd, a post created to maintain a command structure in southern Germany, which faced being split in two by the Allied advance. Six days later Kesselring surrendered to the American forces.

Kesselring leaving a headquarters in winter 1943–44, followed by Generalleutnant Richard Heidrich, commander of 1. Fallschirmjäger-Division, sporting on his left cuff the Kreta cuff title which he earned for his role during the battle for Crete in May 1941. (Count Ernesto G. Vitetti)

Albert Kesselring spent seven years and almost five months in captivity, first as a prisoner of war and then as a convict; he was taken as a witness first to the Nuremberg trial and then to the Dachau process against the Luftwaffe physicians who carried out medical experiments on prisoners. Ill health meant that he did not appear at the Malmedy trial of SS officers responsible for the shooting of US prisoners. He was tried for the killing of 335 Italian

Generalfeldmarschall Wolfram von Richthofen's advanced command post at Anzio, February 1944. As commander of VIII Flieger Korps, the air support command of the Luftwaffe, Richthofen served under Kesselring's command in both 1940 and 1941. (Piero Crociani)

hostages in reprisal for the death of 33 policemen during a partisan attack on 23 March 1944, and on 6 May 1947 he was sentenced to death. It was commuted to life imprisonment after protests from high-ranking Allied commanders (including Churchill), and was reduced to 20 years in 1948. Hospitalized on 15 July 1952, on 23 October Kesselring was released on medical grounds and moved to Bad Nauheim. In 1952 he became leader of the veterans' association Stahlhelm, which he left in 1960; in 1953 he published his memoirs, *Soldat bis zum letzen Tag* (*Soldier to the last day*), followed in 1955 by *Gedanken zum Zweiten Weltkrieg* (*Thoughts on World War II*). He died on 15 July 1960.

HOUR OF DESTINY

The Chief of Staff

Kesselring shortly after his surrender to the Americans on 8 May 1945, when he was Oberbefehlshaber Süd. This was a command created when it became clear that the Allied and Soviet advances would split Germany in two and was matched by an equivalent command in northern Germany. (Count Ernesto G. Vitetti)

Some commentators have assumed that shortly after he took over Wever's position as Chief of Staff of the Luftwaffe in 1936, Kesselring made the decision to cancel the long-range strategic bomber project, thus hampering development in this particular field and destroying Wever's carefully laid plans. But it is worth remembering just how difficult it was to build an air force from scratch, especially given the international restrictions on German rearmament. In 1933 there was practically no German aeroplane industry at all, a situation aggravated by the lack of raw material and the amount of time (at least four years) required to develop and put into production a new model of aircraft. In the early years there were many attempts to get projects to the developmental stage, but by 1936 attempts there was more rationalization and a clear doctrine and a strategy were also developed.

In 1935 Wever summarized the role of the Luftwaffe in his *Luftkriegführung* (conduct of the air war). While stressing the need for maximum flexibility, he also emphasized the role within the overall context of the German war: the air force was to achieve and maintain air superiority over the enemy air forces, while offering support to both the army and the navy, two factors that could not be separated. A strategic air war was contemplated only if necessary and if it could be won.

Germany was not in a position to develop a plan for a strategic air war in the same way as Great Britain or even as theorized in Italy by Giulio Douhet, for both these countries enjoyed a natural protection of their borders that Germany did not have. For Germany, close inter-service cooperation was the best means of both attack and defence. Wever began a four-engine, long-range strategic bomber

A German soldier inspects French bombers destroyed on the ground. The Luftwaffe's greatly inflated estimates of the damage inflicted to the enemy air forces both in Poland in 1939 and in the West in May–June 1940 led to an overestimation of its own capabilities against Britain. (Private collection)

project under the name 'Uralbomber', but before his death the restrictions imposed both by technical difficulties (under-powered engines and excessive fuel consumption), and the decision to develop a Luftwaffe able to closely cooperate with the other services, made this project untenable. As the German historian Horst Boog showed, the decision to cancel the 'Uralbomber' had been made in May 1936 in favour of a 'fast bomber' (eventually the Junkers Ju 88). Wever's death on 3 June prevented him from rubber-stamping the decision, and it was left to his successor to do so. With Göring's support, Kesselring cancelled the Junkers Ju 89 and Dornier Do 19 four-engined bomber programmes on 29 April 1937. What might be regarded as a lack of foresight was in fact a dire necessity; for every four-engine bomber, two-and-a-half twin-engine aircraft could be built.

Kesselring's role as an air strategist is in fact more complicated than might be assumed. First, apart from Wever, there was hardly a single person within the newly formed Luftwaffe with a clear view of its role. Some, like Göring, had been fighter pilots during World War I and many others were ex-army officers, which made them more inclined to consider the Luftwaffe as an army support force. Second, in 1935–36 decisions had to be made that would affect the Luftwaffe's development and shape in the years to come, and required co-operation between the air staff (the Luftkommandoamt) and the Air Ministry (Reichs Luftfahrt Ministerium), most notably the state secretary, Ernst Milch. In some respects Kesselring influenced matters in a positive way, in some others not.

In 1935 the Luftwaffe had some 1,800 aircraft, which were mostly obsolete. Modernization from 1936 produced some 2,900 modern aircraft, which became available in 1938, when limited resources prevented further expansion. Without a doubt, Kesselring's influence related to the experience of German troops in the Spanish Civil War. The first German aircraft, including 20 Junkers Ju 52 (used to transfer troops from Morocco to Spain), arrived in Spain in August 1936, the first part of what became the Legion Condor. Led by Wolfram von Richthofen, this unit acquired valuable experience that eventually shaped the Luftwaffe in the early years of World War II.

Lack of sources make details scarce, but it is clear that Kesselring placed an emphasis on organization, administration, training and supply, most notably in the use of transport aircraft. Kesselring advocated the creation of the Messerschmitt Bf 110-equipped *Zerstörergeschwader* (destroyer wings) that led to the separation between the light, single-engine 'defence fighters' and the heavy twin-engine 'escort fighters'. He also worked for the eventual creation of a real air force staff and underlined the importance of the Luftwaffe's role in support of the ground forces. Even though Wever had enjoyed the title of 'chief of the air staff', until 1937 there was no Luftwaffe staff, but rather a Luftkommandoamt directly subordinated to the state secretary. Wever had drawn up a new organization, but it was Kesselring who implemented it.

The Luftwaffe staff (Generalstab der Luftwaffe) was formed on 1 June 1937 and was no longer subordinate to the state secretary, only bound to co-operate with him. Kesselring undoubtedly regarded the basic function of the Luftwaffe as a support for the army, and he never made a secret of that. In the summer of 1941, for example, while commanding the Luftflotte 2 on the Eastern Front, he demonstrated many times that he understood the air force's role in support of frontline troops. He offered unconditional support to reinforce the army's ground war tactics and ordered the air units and Flak (anti-aircraft) commanders to treat requests from the Army as though they came directly from him. Kesselring may have begun his professional career as an army officer, but after 1933 he genuinely worked in the best interests of the Luftwaffe. Unlike other Luftwaffe commanders, Kesselring stressed the need for the newly created Luftwaffe field divisions (divisions of Luftwaffe personnel who fought as infantry) to be subordinated to the army, simply because this was the only way to ensure their proper training. This demonstrates Kesselring's good sense as an air commander and encapsulates why he generally enjoyed success in supporting the army during ground campaigns, but was less successful when facing a strategic air war.

The air commander

Kesselring's role as a *Luftflotte* commander demonstrates that some successes were achieved only by a narrow margin. In September 1939, when the war against Poland broke out, the Luftwaffe had 4,161 aircraft, including 1,179 fighters, 1,180 bombers, 366 Stuka (dive bombers), 40 ground-attack and 552 transport. Not all of them were deployed against Poland, with Kesselring's Luftflotte 1 (in north-eastern Germany) having 1,105 combat aircraft and Alexander Löhr's Luftflotte 4 (in south-eastern Germany) having 729, with 262 directly assigned to the army, for a total of 2,096. The Polish air force had about 400 aircraft, including 159 fighters, 118 ground-attack and 36 medium bombers. Contrary to popular belief they were not destroyed on the ground at the start of the German campaign. On 1 September only five airfields were attacked by the Luftwaffe and 56 per cent of missions were flown in support of the army and the navy, with only 44 per cent against the Polish air forces. On 2 September the Luftwaffe flew

370 missions in support of ground forces and only 110 in direct air combat against the Polish air forces or its airfields (and the whereabouts of Poland's bombers was unknown). Even though the Luftwaffe stated that air supremacy had been achieved by 3 September and that the Polish air force no longer existed, Polish bombers and ground-attack aircraft continued to harass German troops until the 16th. Their tactics (the use of small groups of two or three aircraft) greatly lessened their effectiveness, however. At the end of the campaign the Luftwaffe had lost 285 planes destroyed, and 279 damaged beyond repair.

Top brass during the Battle of Britain gathered at Cap Gris Nez; from left to right generals Hans Jeschonnek (Chief of Air Staff), Albert Kesselring, Wilhelm Speidel (Chief of Staff, Luftflotte 2), Bruno Loerzer (commander, II Flieger Korps). (Count Ernesto G. Vitetti)

These figures show that the Luftwaffe did not achieve victory easily: they had to fight hard and the same was true in the campaign in the West in the summer of 1940. By 10 May 1940 the Luftwaffe had greatly increased its strength, with a total of 5,446 aircraft, of which 3,864 were combat aircraft. 3,578 of these were deployed on the West (1,563 bombers, 376 Stuka, 49 ground-attack, 1,279 single-engine and 311 twin-engine fighters), although only 2,589 of them were serviceable.

The Allies had more aircraft: the French had 3,097; the RAF 1,150 deployed in France; and 140 Belgian and 82 Dutch aircraft gave a total of 4,469. The RAF had a further 540 fighters and 310 bombers deployed in the British Isles. The German attack started in the same way as the invasion of Poland the previous September. The Luftwaffe attacked enemy airfields, but there was no annihilating blow and only some 60 enemy aircraft were destroyed on the ground.

The Allied reaction was weak, however, and on 12 May the Luftwaffe turned mainly to ground support. According to German claims, between 10 and 13 May 879 enemy aircraft had been destroyed, with the bulk (560) destroyed on the ground, 215 destroyed in air combat and 104 shot down by anti-aircraft fire. German losses were 183 aircraft lost (including 105 bombers, 14 Stuka, 35 single and 13 twin-engine fighters), plus another 131 Junkers Ju 52 transport planes. Exaggerated as these figures may appear (in fact only 219 destroyed enemy aircraft were confirmed), it is true that in the first days of the offensive, the Allied air effort was almost an exact replica of the Polish one; attacks were performed by small groups, with the French fighters defensively patrolling assigned areas, rather than attacking the Germans. The main effort was made by RAF bombers, bravely but with scarce results; in two days the Advanced Air Striking Force was down from 135 to 72 serviceable aircraft, and the attempt to destroy the bridges at

One of Kesselring's last inspection trips to Tunisia before the surrender. At centre Generaloberst Hans-Jürgen von Arnim, commander of Heeresgruppe Afrika since March 1943 after he commanded the 5. Panzer Armee, to the right Field Marshal Ugo Cavallero, the Italian Chief of General Staff. (Count Ernesto G. Vitetti)

Sedan on 14 May ended with a loss rate of 56 per cent, which eroded British morale. By 14 May the Luftwaffe had achieved air superiority in the north-west of France.

Kesselring's Luftflotte 2 included a special command, Flieger Korps z.b.V. 2 (2nd Air Corps for special purposes) operating in Holland. The IV and VIII Flieger Korps were led by Richthofen and included the bulk of Luftwaffe's ground-attack units, and the II Flak Korps. Total strength was 1,836 aircraft (1,285 serviceable) and on 10 May Luftflotte 2 attacked airfields in Holland, Belgium and northern France. It moved to air interdiction in the Hague–Rotterdam–Moerdijk region in Holland, as well as in western Belgium and the north of France between Cambrai and Antwerp. Kesselring was nominally responsible for airborne operations in Holland and at Eben Emael, although details had been worked out by Hitler and Göring without consulting him, and the result was a compromise solution that created confusion in the chain of command. With the Dutch and Belgian air forces practically destroyed on the first day, from 11 May Luftflotte 2 was mainly occupied with screening the northern flank of the offensive. On 12 May VIII Flieger Korps was detached to support the attack at Sedan and it was permanently detached to Luftflotte 3 on the 16th, replaced by I Flieger Korps. On 14 May Göring ordered the bombing of Rotterdam while surrender negotiations were still ongoing and the Dutch finally surrendered on 20 May when the Panzers reached the Channel coast and the Luftwaffe reckoned that it had achieved air supremacy. Between 15 and 20 May the Luftwaffe reported the loss of 164 aircraft (with total losses since 10 May amounting to 527 aircraft destroyed or heavily damaged) against claims for a total of 564 enemy aircraft destroyed; 285 in air combat, 34 by anti-aircraft fire and 245 on the ground.

From 20 May Luftflotte 2, now engaged in ground support, increased its activity against naval targets in the Channel, but on the same day, when enemy fighter activity increased, it discovered a large number of enemy aircraft in the airfields in the western sector, which were not attacked immediately. Attention soon shifted to other targets. The history of Dunkirk and Operation *Dynamo* need not be repeated here, apart from Göring's claim on 25 May that the Luftwaffe could deal with the pocket alone. Consequently, the advance of the Panzer units was halted.

Kesselring realized that the responsibility of preventing the Allied evacuation remained entirely with his pilots, and his complaints to Göring clearly summarized the situation. Apart from Richthofen's VIII Flieger Korps, now redeploying in the Cambrai-Saint-Quentin area, all other units were based in Germany, about 300km (186 miles) east of Dunkirk. Hampered by bad weather, persistent attacks from the RAF and a decline in the number of serviceable aircraft, (IV Flieger Korps was down to 50–60 per cent, and units like Kampfgeschwader 4 down to one-third of their strength) Kesselring made the best of a bad job. The fight for Dunkirk between 26 May and 4 June by Luftflotte 2 and VIII Flieger Korps was the first real strategic battle fought by the Luftwaffe, and it revealed its weaknesses. Targets were shifted, with the first series of attacks (26 to 29 May) carried out against harbours and naval targets. Bad weather forced a temporary cessation of action on 30 May, and from the 31st attacks focused on troop concentrations and the shore. The massive air raid against Paris on 3 June practically put an end to the battle and cost the Luftwaffe 132 aircraft against the 145 lost by home-based RAF units. Bad weather, in particular on 28–31 May, greatly hampered the Luftwaffe's activity, which coincided with the peak of the Allied evacuation effort.

The Battle of Britain

In June the French Air Force was to receive some 668 new fighters and 355 bombers, but the decision to send air units to north-west Africa reduced the impact of these reinforcements and, after early serious opposition, by 9 June the French Air Force reduced its efforts. The German attack across the Somme began on 5 June, and on the 22nd France surrendered. The Luftwaffe claimed a total of 1,336 enemy aircraft destroyed between 3 and 24 June, to add to the total of 3,491 enemy aircraft destroyed between 10 May and 3 June. Actual figures give 892 aircraft lost by the French and 1,029 lost by the RAF, but the Luftwaffe's losses were higher: figures vary, but overall losses in May–June 1940 (all theatres and all types) give 1,428 destroyed and 488 damaged, with details for the campaign in the West giving a loss of 1,239 combat aircraft (including damaged) – 635 bombers, 147 Stuka and close support, and 457 fighters. Taking into account the weaknesses shown by Allied air forces, in particular the French, it is clear that the Luftwaffe fought and won a hard victory. Without the decision to concentrate on army support this victory might not have been achieved at all.

This is only one side of the coin; in the summer of 1940 there was practically no real strategic air force anywhere in the world, and it took years for the RAF and the USAAF to build one. A lack of strategic vision is only one

Destroyed aircraft of the Soviet Air Force. In the early stages of Barbarossa the Luftwaffe was able to destroy larger numbers than ever on the ground, even though that only temporarily won them air supremacy.
(Nik Cornish at Stavka)

Kesselring at the headquarters of Panzergruppe Afrika in 1942. Kesselring temporarily took command of Gruppe Crüwell on 29 May 1942, therefore placing himself under Rommel's command if only for a few days. (Count Ernesto G. Vitetti)

of the reasons behind the Luftwaffe's failure in the Battle of Britain. Another reason is provided by the figures given above, which show the extent of the strain and attrition on German aircrews and machines between May and September 1940. Compared to the Luftwaffe's fighting strength in the West in May 1940, on 20 July the combined strength of Luftflotte 2 and 3 was only 2,651 combat aircraft (1,502/841 operational) of which 1,131 were bombers (769), 316 Stuka (248), 809 single-engined fighters (656), and 246 twin-engined fighters (168). There were an additional 342 combat aircraft (259 operational) under Luftflotte 5 in Norway, with 129 bombers (95 operational) and 34 twin-engined fighters (32 operational). Even though numbers had increased by 10 August, with a total of 2,898 combat aircraft, 2,277 operational (1,360 bombers, 998 operational; 406 Stuka, 316 operational; 813 single-engined fighters, 702 operational; 319 twin-engined fighters, 261 operational), it is clear that the Luftwaffe had far from recovered from the attrition suffered in the campaign of May–June 1940.

The Luftwaffe's situation was worsened by other factors. Faulty intelligence meant that the Luftwaffe attacked the wrong airfields that were not part of Fighter Command. There was an overestimation of the Luftwaffe's capabilities, although it soon became clear that a large portion of the combat aircraft, namely the Junkers Ju 87 Stuka dive-bomber and the twin-engined Messerschmitt Bf 110 fighter were inadequate in this kind of air warfare. There was also a shortage of heavy bombs (500kg or more) and sea mines had to be used as substitutes.

Given these factors, German planning proved dramatically short-sighted, if not simply wrong. On 25 July the air staff rejected a plan drawn up by Luftflotte 2 and 3 for an attack on Britain. It was revised and submitted to Göring during the 1 August conference at The Hague. Göring and his commanders, Kesselring and Sperrle, favoured different approaches. Kesselring and Sperrle advised launching a strategic air war against the RAF, that included attacks on aircraft production facilities, but Göring demanded a blitzkrieg-style war similar to the attacks on Poland and France. Göring was firmly convinced that air superiority could be achieved in five days, and air supremacy in 13 days, a period that would be followed by a series of attacks advancing north sector by sector. The following day Göring issued his directive and on 6 August another conference was held at Carinhall, Göring's residence, to prepare for the *Adlertag* (Eagle Day).

When the first phase of the Battle of Britain began on 8 August Luftflotte 2 represented the bulk of the Luftwaffe in the West, with I and II Flieger Korps and 821 bombers, 74 Stukas, 574 single-engined and 190 twin-engined fighters. So far, Kesselring had used Stukas to attack convoys in the Channel and the fighters to engage in dogfights with the Hurricanes and Spitfires of the RAF, with fairly good results. His tactical use of fighter aircraft reveals the extent of the Luftwaffe's overestimation of its capabilities, however. Sticking to the concept of 'defence fighters' and 'escort fighters', Kesselring asked his fighter units to provide close escort support to the bombers, including the expectation that they would follow the Stukas in their dives, as well as engaging enemy fighter aircraft. This problem should have been solved by the use of the twin-engined Bf 110 for close escort and the single-engined Bf 109 for fighter engagement. Fighter commander Theo Osterkamp suggested a mixed use of the two aircraft, a proposal approved by Kesselring who rejected mixing *Jäger* (single-engine fighters) and *Zerstörer* (twin-engine ones) units for 'colour' reasons.

Adlertag did not begin well. Göring ordered a postponement of the attacks because of bad weather, but the message did not reach every unit. Kesselring greatly overestimated the effects of the attacks on the radar stations, as well as those against the RAF's airfields. On 15 August, after another conference at Carinhall, Kesselring decided to use heavy escorted raids on fewer, selected airfields, along with fighter missions. At the end of the first phase on 18 August the Luftwaffe's losses amounted to 358 aircraft lost, plus 102 damaged, while the RAF lost 165 aircraft destroyed (plus 25 on the ground) and 50 damaged (plus eight on the ground).

On 19 August there was a change of strategy following another conference at Carinhall: Sperrle's Luftflotte 3 was to hand over the bulk of its fighters to Kesselring's Luftflotte 2 and concentrate on night raids. Because of its heavy losses, the Ju 87 Stuka was to be withdrawn from the battle and, on specific instructions from Göring, fighters were to closely escort the bombers. The Bf 110s also suffered heavy losses and it was even suggested that they should be escorted by the Bf 109. It is hard to evaluate the actual strength increase of Luftflotte 2, but on 7 September it included 764 bombers and 669 fighters, plus 163 Stukas and 184 twin-engined fighters. With Kesselring now in charge, the Luftwaffe increased its attacks against RAF airfields and the situation improved, with the Luftwaffe losing 375/382 aircraft (plus 101 damaged) against the RAF's 273 destroyed (plus 17 on the ground) and 53 damaged (plus 13 on the ground) up to 5 September.

The real turning point in the battle was a result of faulty intelligence, and it is ironic that Kesselring, a commander who insisted on accurate intelligence, suffered as a result.

Hermann Göring and Bruno Loerzer during the Battle of Britain. Although neither a skilled nor competent commander, Loerzer was in command of II Flieger Korps from October 1939 until 23 February 1943, serving under Kesselring. (Count Ernesto G. Vitetti)

Two twin-engine Messerschmitt Bf 110 fighter aircraft in sand camouflage flying over the Mediterranean. The one in the foreground belongs to Zerstörergeschwader 26, while the one in background carries no insignia and an unidentified unit numbering. (*Signal*)

By late August Luftwaffe intelligence suggested that Fighter Command was a spent force, and claimed a total of 1,115 enemy aircraft destroyed, with no more than 150–300 fighters left in England. During the conference at The Hague on 3 September, Kesselring used these wildly optimistic figures to advise Göring to launch the second phase and attack London, which would force the RAF to commit its last reserves. Sperrle disagreed, but on 30 August Göring had already advised Hitler to begin attacks on London. The order was issued on 5 September, but ten days later the Battle of Britain was practically lost, even though air raids continued for months. Between July and September 1940 the Luftwaffe lost a grand total of 1,636 aircraft destroyed and 697 damaged, but this was only the end of the beginning.

In May 1941 Kesselring redeployed to the East and from 22 June Luftflotte 2 successfully provided air support for the advancing armies. Supporting Heeresgruppe Mitte, Kesselring's aircraft attacked the enemy airfields within a 300km (186 mile) radius, claiming the destruction of 1,570 enemy aircraft by 28 June. Claims, both in terms of aircraft and land targets, steadily increased with the advance of the German army. It is worth noting how, between June and November 1941, the single II Flieger Korps dropped more than 23,000 tons of bombs, compared to the 40,000 tons dropped by the entire Luftwaffe on Britain between July and December 1940. But Kesselring's time in the East came soon to an end, and on 28 November Luftflotte 2 was already in the Mediterranean.

Battle of Britain

The Battle of Britain was the first strategic air war in history. On paper the forces were uneven, with the Luftwaffe holding the advantage of superior numbers and tactics. In reality the RAF enjoyed the advantage of fighting in defence, with the help of radar, while the Luftwaffe suffered not only from the losses of the previous months, but also from several deficiencies in the fields of intelligence and aircraft. The only suitable fighter, the Messerschmitt Bf 109, had a limited range and the bombers, like the Heinkel He 111 shown here, were only able to carry limited amounts of bombs and soon became extremely vulnerable to RAF fighters such as the Supermarine Spitfire Mk II. Soon the German fighters were compelled to close escort the German bombers, which further reduced their range. Here we see a Bf 109 fighter from Jagdgeschwader 3 (fighter wing) fighting with Spitfires from No. 19 Squadron while escorting Heinkel bombers.

Junkers Ju 52 transport planes en route to Tunisia, November 1942. Kesselring complained about the losses suffered by transports during the attempts to resupply Stalingrad in winter 1942–43, and these aircraft played a major role in the Mediterranean. (Andrea Molinari)

Oberbefehlshaber Süd

German intervention in the Mediterranean in 1941 was not only belated, following the Italian cry for help after their defeats, but also fragmentary. In spite of Rommel's initial successes, in autumn 1941 it was clear that the whole North African and Mediterranean area was in a critical situation, caused largely by the British interdiction of the sea supply lanes. Freighter losses increased steadily from September and peaked in November. Although the bulk of German armed forces were fighting on the Eastern Front, Kesselring was appointed as Oberbefehlshaber Süd (Commander-in-Chief South). He retained command of Luftflotte 2, which was transferred from the Eastern Front along with II Flieger Korps, with the task of regaining the initiative in the Mediterranean, specifically to obtain air supremacy in the central Mediterranean, to close it to British convoys, and to eliminate the problem of Malta. Kesselring was ordered to work in close cooperation with the other German forces in the theatre, as well as with Italian forces and the navies of both countries. Kesselring answered directly to Mussolini, who issued his directives through the Comando Supremo (Italian Chief o General Staff); to Göring in all the Luftwaffe matters; and to the Oberkommando der Wehrmacht (OKW, the German General Staff) in all strategic matters.

Just another conference to discuss the vital matter of supplies to Rommel's forces in North Africa; from the left Rommel, Kesselring and Vice-admiral Eberhard Weichold who, as commander of Deutsche Marinekommando Italien (German Naval Command Italy), was responsible for the sea transports. (Count Ernesto G. Vitetti)

Malta was at the centre of the problem. Used as a base by the British, it enabled them to blockade German supply routes to Libya. Kesselring initiated night raids on Malta from December 1941, which enabled the Germans to re-open the sea lanes, and eventually made Rommel's drive to Gazala in January 1942 possible. On 31 December 1941 Kesselring issued his own directives intended to eliminate Malta as an air and sea base while retaining the decision when to start the offensive. The delay in the redeployment of II Flieger Korps units frustrated both him and Mussolini, who was keen for air attacks to start in February. The start of the offensive on Malta was scheduled for March, even though attacks on the island by II Flieger Korps in February had already forced RAF Blenheim bombers to redeploy to Egypt.

On 12 March 1942 Kesselring held a conference at Catania airfield clearly outlining how the problem of Malta was to be solved: the island was to be annihilated with a series of air strikes, starting with the destruction of the enemy anti-aircraft artillery, then the airfields, and eventually the harbours and all the naval targets. In March II Flieger Korps flew 4,881 missions, which increased in frequency once the offensive started on 20 March. Until the end of this phase on 28 April, II Flieger Korps' units performed as well as they had during the Battle of Britain, with a total of 11,819 missions flown (5,807 bombers, 5,667 fighters and 345 recce) and 6,557 tons of bombs dropped.

Results were immediate: in January 1942 Malta received 21,000 tons of supplies, but Luftwaffe attacks destroyed two major convoys, *MF 5* on 12–15 February, and *MW 10* on 22–26 March. With minimal supplies, Malta was almost annihilated as an air and sea base; the 60 aircraft that remained in February managed to sink only one-fifth of the Axis tonnage that had been sunk in the last five months of 1941, while in early April all surface vessels left the island, followed mid-month by the submarines of the 10th Flotilla.

This was a victory, but was also clearly flawed, for it provided only temporary respite. In fact, Kesselring knew on 17 March that many units of Luftflotte 2 would be deployed to the Eastern Front from April. Overall strength suffered; Luftlotte had a total strength of 712 aircraft of all types on 4 April, and 711 on 20 May, but the number of bombers had declined from 207 to 189, day fighters from 232 to 189, and Stuka from 80 to 64. On 4 April the strength of II Flieger Korps was 434 but this had shrunk to 216 aircraft by 20 May. Insufficient operational levels and the multiplication of duties, such as the need to attack British convoys, as dictated by Luftflotte 2 directive of 20 February 1942, and the simultaneous requirement to protect the Axis convoys further aggravated the problem of declining numbers. Moreover, there was very little air co-operation with the Italian air force. Given the different performance of their aircraft, not to mention the use of different communication systems, the Italians could offer support, but joint operations were simply not possible, and this was intensified by their fierce independence. Consequently, the Italian air force only flew 791 missions against Malta in February 1942, followed by a further 806 in March and 858 in April, compared to a total of 18,999 flown by the Germans.

By the end of the offensive in April, it should have been clear that the problem of Malta was

German paratroopers of Kampfgruppe Koch, Fallschirmjäger-Regiment 5, at Medjez el Bab, Tunisia, November 1942. From the end of 1942 *Fallschirmjäger* units played a leading role in the battles fought in Tunisia and in Italy. (Count Ernesto G. Vitetti)

A Messerschmitt Bf 110 twin-engine fighter in Sicily, 1942, just transferred from the Eastern Front. A failure during the Battle of Britain, it was to prove its worth in the Mediterranean thanks to its range and endurance. (*Signal*)

anything but solved, and that it was only a matter of time before it would resurface. Kesselring's optimistic view led him to different conclusions, however. While stressing the need to capture the island, he did not regard Malta as a long-term threat. Following the redeployment of II Flieger Korps, on 7 May an order was issued to continue the air war against the island. The Luftwaffe was to carry out a blockade, while the Italians would attack Malta itself. In May the Italian effort reached its peak with 1,597 missions, while II Flieger Korps flew 3,136, a figure that shrank to 1,373 in June, when the Italians flew 1,520 missions. There were serious losses among the ships of Operation *Harpoon*, the convoys sent to Malta on 13–16 June, but Malta was once more resupplied with 25,000 tons. By then the fate of the island had already been sealed.

Malta or Tobruk?

Italian planning for the seizure of Malta started in December 1941, but even by February 1942 General Cavallero (the Italian Chief of General Staff) had not taken a clear position on the matter. On 9 March, OKW asked Kesselring to ascertain the extent of Italian planning and two days later a note confirmed the Italian schedule for an assault to take place in July. Kesselring was not concerned about the delay, which allowed more time to prepare and would eventually make the seizure of Malta easier than that of Crete in April 1941, where the Germans suffered serious casualties.

On 17 March Kesselring told Cavallero that Luftflotte 2 units were to be redeployed to the Eastern Front. Between 9 and 15 March a series of meetings was held in Libya to discuss the forthcoming offensive against Tobruk, which,

1. Day X: air attacks start on the Interdiction Line.
2. Day X: units of the German 7. Flieger and Italian Folgore airborne divisions are dropped in the Dingli–Zurrieq area in three waves during the day.
3. Day X: German gliderborne units attack Fort Benghisa and land in the Kalafrana area.
4. Day X+1: Landing in the 'Famagosta' (southern coast) area, led by one San Marco battalion and elements of the seaborne Blackshirts brigade.
5. Day X+1: elements of Blackshirts brigade land in the 'Larnaca' (Kalafrana) area.
6. Day X+1: after the initial assault the Friuli Division is landed at 'Larnaca' three hours later.
7. Day X+1: follow-up units are the Raggruppamento Corazzato (RaCo) and the Livorno Division.
8. Day X+1: the Friuli Division advances toward Kalafrana seizing the Hal Far airport and attacking the Marsa Scirocco area.
9. Day X+2: the La Spezia airlanding division arrives at the Hal Far airport.
10. Day X+2: the Assietta and Napoli divisions land at 'Famagosta' to relieve the paratroopers.
11. Day X+2: The Livorno Division advances toward Zejtun.
12. Day X+2: The seizure of the eastern tip of Malta is completed.
13. One regiment of the Superga Division lands west of 'Jaffa' (east of St Paul's Bay), the Assietta and Napoli divisions advance inland.
14. The Assietta and Napoli divisions advance northwards, linking up with the Superga regiment north of Mosla.
15. Day X+1: The bulk of Superga Division, broken down along with one San Marco marine infantry battalion and one seaborne Blackshirt battalion into eight assault groups, lands at Gozo establishing five beachheads.
16. Day X+1: advance inland from the beachheads.
17. Day X+2: Seizure of Victoria and of the eastern tip of Gozo.
18. Mopping-up operations at Gozo.

The planned assault on Malta, 1942

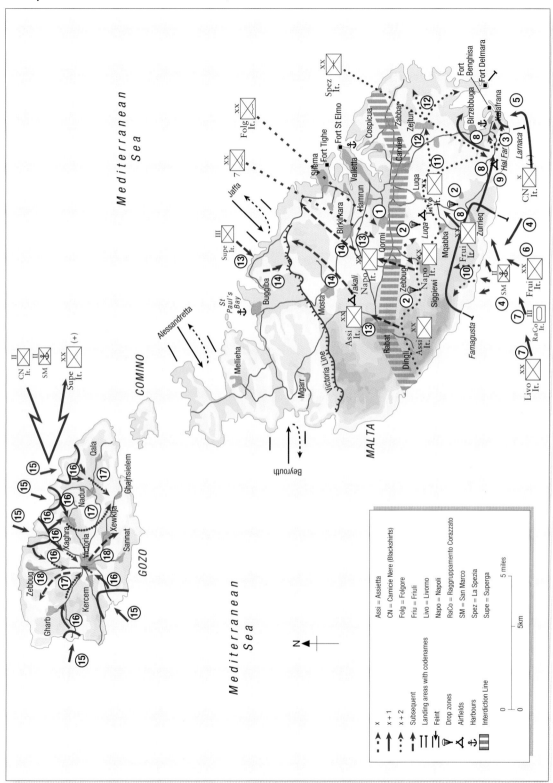

Key:
- x
- x + 1
- x + 2
- Subsequent
- Landing areas with codenames
- Feint
- Drop zones
- Airfields
- Harbours
- Interdiction Line

Assi = Assietta
CN = Camicie Nere (Blackshirts)
Folg = Folgore
Friu = Friuli
Livo = Livorno
Napo = Napoli
RaCo = Raggruppamento Corazzato
SM = San Marco
Spez = La Spezia
Supe = Superga

Kesselring inspecting a *Fallschirmjäger* unit in Italy, summer 1943. Two new divisions were formed between summer and winter 1943, which coincided with the German build-up in the Mediterranean and Italy. (Count Ernesto G. Vitetti)

in Cavallero's view, did not effect the planned seizure of Malta. Mussolini told Rommel that he was determined that the attack would take place in July–August, after the attack against Tobruk. On 19 March Cavallero openly told the German military attaché Rintelen that German support was vital for the seizure of Malta.

On 21 March Kesselring had a meeting with Hitler, to whom he submitted the Italian requests and thus began the German planning for Operation *Herkules*, the codename for the capture of Malta. On 7–8 April Kesselring and Rommel decided that the attack against Tobruk was to take place in May–June, partly because the weather would be cooler than in July, and partly because British forces were already preparing an offensive. The seizure of Malta was to take place either before Rommel's attack, as a *coup de main* strike, despite Italian opposition to this plan, or else after it, with a full-scale assault.

On 11–12 April Kesselring told Mussolini and Cavallero about the meetings and about the redeployment of the German air units, remarking that Malta was now unusable by the British as a naval base even though it could still be used as an air base. Mussolini asked that a joint Italian-German staff be formed to plan the operation.

The staff was formed on 13 April under the command of the Italian General Gandin (probably chosen because he spoke good German), but it was clear by 29–30 April that the seizure of Malta could not take place until July. Furthermore, the Italians submitted a series of requests to the Germans for military support, including a parachute division (7. Flieger-Division, later 1. Fallschirmjäger) with transport planes, 25–30 tanks, 50 landing crafts, 200 Ju 52 transport planes, gliders, 8,000 containers for air supply, and more than 50,000 tons of fuel.

On 21 April Hitler decided to support Rommel's attack against Tobruk, even though orders were given to send to the Mediterranean one assault engineer battalion, two paratrooper battalions (with planes to carry only one of them) and the landing craft requested by the Italians. On the same day, Kesselring told Cavallero about Hitler's 'green light' for Rommel's attack and the seizure of Malta, and stressed how in two weeks the German air units in central Mediterranean would shrink by 50 per cent in bombers and 30–40 per cent in fighters. On 29–30 April Hitler and Mussolini met, along with Kesselring and Cavallero, to discuss the strategic situation. On this occasion Hitler agreed with Rommel's view, giving priority to the attack against Tobruk and an offensive against Egypt, which was to be followed by the capture of Malta in June–July. On 19 May Kesselring's staff submitted a first plan for Operation *Herkules* based on a series of landings in the southern part of Malta, followed by the capture of the eastern part of the island, a scheme that was revised on the 31st to include an attack force totalling some 100,000 men.

On 26–27 May Rommel's attack against the Gazala Line started and, after fierce fighting, Tobruk was captured on 20–21 June. By 23 June Rommel's spearheads were close to the Egyptian frontier and he sought permission to proceed with the offensive into Egypt. Mussolini rejected the idea and, with Cavallero's support, wanted to stop the advance at the frontier while Malta was captured. However, at midnight on 24 June, Rommel was authorized to advance into Egypt, and troops scheduled for use in Malta were sent to North Africa.

Operation *Herkules* was eventually abandoned, and Rommel's advance was to halt in July in front of El Alamein, partly because of logistical difficulties. During the many meetings that debated the fate of Malta, Kesselring had repeated his belief that Malta must first be neutralized in order to protect German supply routes, and only then should an offensive be launched in North Africa.

A Panzer IV tank of 16. Panzer-Division at Salerno, September 1943, just before the counterattack. The use of armour on the German side in the Italian campaign was always limited and often unwise, with heavy losses suffered because of Allied naval artillery. (Filippo Cappellano)

In that same month it became clear that German air superiority on Malta was lost, and by the end of the month the British 10th Submarine Flotilla had returned to the island. On 1 July Kesselring launched a new air offensive against Malta that ended in a failure, and was recalled on the 23rd because of crippling losses. The complete loss of air superiority in the Mediterranean to the Allies was now only a matter of time. Although in mid-August the convoys of Operation *Pedestal* were attacked, 47,000 tons of supplies reached Malta and ensured the island's survival through the winter. That same month, II Flieger Korps flew 618 missions, that is 33 per cent of a total of 1,847, to escort convoys to North Africa, but even this did not prevent the deterioration of Rommel's supply situation between August and October 1942. On 24 August II Flieger Korps issued an order for the defence of Sicily, and the Blitz launched on Malta the following October practically put an end to the strategic air war in the Mediterranean. With 196 bombers (119 operational) and 107 fighters (78) operational, II Flieger Korps had the edge over RAF forces based on Malta, which had only 140 aircraft (130 operational), but shortly after the Blitz started on 10 October, Kesselring ordered the fighters resume bomber-escort duties. The new offensive was called off on the 17th, with the Luftwaffe flying 2,089 missions along with 846 Italian ones. The Axis forces lost air superiority on Malta and from then Luftflotte 2 flew defensive operations.

Tunisia and Sicily

On 4 November 1942 Rommel began to withdraw from El Alamein after the defeat inflicted by Montgomery's Eighth Army, and four days later the Allied forces landed in French North Africa as part of Operation *Torch*. Facing a completely different strategic situation, Kesselring reacted promptly. With the agreement of Hitler and Mussolini, he worked to establish a bridgehead to protect Tunisia, with its two deep-water ports and proximity to Sicily, from Allied incursion in the West. On 9 November he sent two groups of Jagdgeschwader 53, the second squadron of Stukageschwader 3 and a company of Luftwaffe field personnel and a Flak platoon under the command of Oberst Harlinghausen. Units destined for Rommel's army, as well as anything else close by, were diverted and sent to Tunisia as part of Gefechtsverband Tunis (Combat Formation Tunis). Part of Fallschirmjäger-Regiment 5 and Kampfgruppe Schirmer were flown to Tunis, eventually seizing the airfield and the town by 12 November. Two days later General Walter Nehring, formerly commander of the Afrika Korps, arrived in Rome with orders to set up a staff directly subordinate to Kesselring, and to create a bridgehead between Tunis and Bizerte; he arrived at Tunis on the 16th to command XC Korps and the following day established two bridgeheads, one at Tunis under Harlinghausen (replaced on the 18th by Oberstleutnant Koch, commander of FJR 5), and the other one at Bizerte under command of Oberstleutnant Stolz (also replaced on 18 November by Oberst von Broich). Although only weak units were available, Nehring ordered them to reconnoitre west but, as early as 17–18 November, advance parties of both Kampfgruppe Witzig from Bizerte and of Kampfgruppe

1. On 11 and 12 November the Tunis and Bizerte bridgeheads are established under command of Oberst Harlinghausen (who formed a *Kampfgruppe* with three coys of a replacement battalion, detachments of Fallschirmjäger-Regiment 5, 14. Kompanie of Panzergrenadier-Regiment 104 and a Flak battery) and Oberst Lederer (forming a *Kampfgruppe* with one coy from the replacement battalion, 4. Kompanie of Panzer-Abteilung 190, 4./Artillerie-Regiment 2 and a battery from Artillerie-Regiment 190); on 14 November XC Corps is formed to control both bridgeheads, becoming 5. Panzer Armee on 9 December.

2. On 18 November Oberstleutnant Koch of Fallschirmjäger-Regiment 5 takes over command of the Tunis bridgehead, while the Bizerte bridgehead (between 16 and 18 November under the command of Oberstleutnant Stolz) is taken over by Oberst von Broich, who commands the newly formed 'Division von Broich'.

3. From 20 November the Tunis Sud bridgehead is formed under Italian command, General Lorenzelli of the Superga Division. On 23 November General Fischer, commander of 10. Panzer-Division, takes over command of Tunis bridgehead from Koch.

4. From 16 November III/Fallschirmjäger-Regiment 5 advances inland toward Medjez el Bab and Bou Arada.

5. 17 November, an advance party of Blade Force (part of the British 78th Division, along with elements of the British 6th Armoured Division and US 1st Armored Division) reaches Medjez el Bab after a two-day march from Algeria, on the 19th they support the local French troops that attack Hauptmann Knoche's III/Fallschirmjäger-Regiment 5. The German advance is checked, but Knoche retains control of Medjez el Bab.

6. 23 November, a reconnaissance party of III/Fallschirm-Jäger-Regiment 5 is thrown back from El Aroussa by units of Blade Force.

7. 17 November, a reconnaissance group from Witzig's XI Fallschirm-Pioniere-Bataillon clashes with the vanguards of British 36th Brigade at Djebel Abiud, the first stage of a battle that ends on the 20th with British troops outmanoeuvring the Germans and compelling them to withdraw east.

8. From 17 November the Allied drive to Tunis and Bizerte consists of two northern prongs, led by the British 36th Brigade (advancing from Bone) and the 1st Parachute Battalion, flown from Algiers to Souk el Arba.

9. The southern prongs were made up of Blade Force, followed by the British 78th Brigade and, from 27 November, by the CCB of US 1st Armored Division.

10. On 18 November a company from the British 1st Parachute Battalion ambushes a German reconnaissance team at Sidi Nsir, another clash follows on the 20th with the 1st Battalion withdrawing on 1–2 December.

11. The advance of the 36th Brigade on 26–28 November, halted at Djefna.

12. The advance of Blade Force on 25–28 November, on the 26th, with a US Armored team spearheading the advance, raided the airfield at Djedeida.

13. The 11th Brigade attacks the German positions at Medjez el Bab on 25 November, forcing the defenders of Fallschirmjäger-Regiment 5 to withdraw on the 26th.

14. 11th Brigade advances to Tebourba on 26 November, and subsequently towards Djedeida on 27–28 November.

15. 29 November, the British 2nd Parachute Battalion is dropped at Depienne, only to face a German roadblock halting its advance, it eventually withdraws on 1 December after an advance to Oudna and west of Tunis.

16. 1–3 December, the Germans counterattack the Allied spearheads at Chouigui and Tebourba with armoured elements (KG Lüder, with one tank company and one platoon of Tiger tanks, KG Hudel with two tank companies) plus the mixed Kampfgruppen Djedeida and Koch, mostly from Fallschirmjäger-Regiment 5; Blade Force withdraws to Tebourba along with the spearheads of 11th Brigade, supported by CCB US 1st Armoured.

The Tunis bridgehead, November 1942

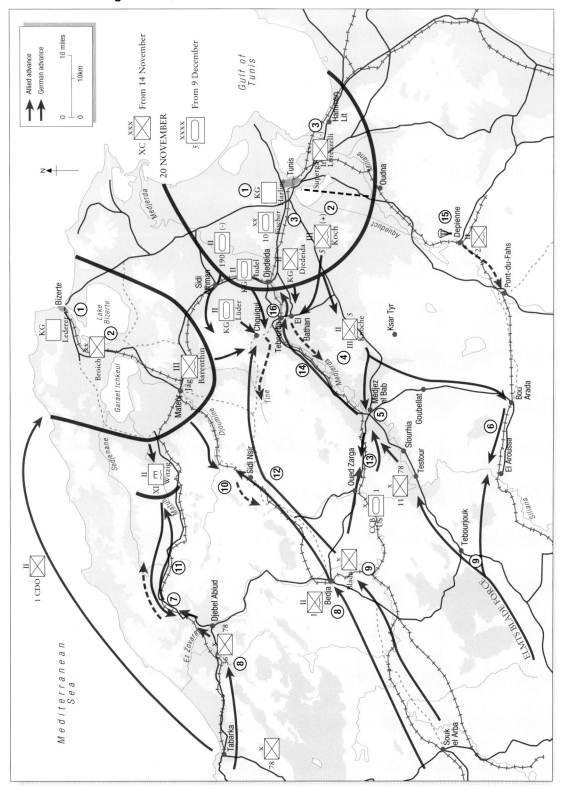

31

Siegfried Westphal leaves the Italian delegation at the conclusion of the surrender negotiation, Rome, 10 September 1943. A skilled and talented staff officer, Westphal's hand was behind the strategic plans for the Italian campaign from 1943. (Piero Crociani)

Schirmer, moving from Tunis, clashed with the advancing British forces and Nehring ordered them to secure their positions. On 20 November, after a fierce battle with the spearheads of the Allied forces, the German paratroopers seized Medjez el Bab.

This allowed Kesselring to bring in more reinforcements, and by 25 November there were about 15,575 Germans and 9,000 Italians in the two bridgeheads. The same day Allied forces under command of General Anderson (commander of British 78th Division, reinforced with elements of US 1st Armored Division) attacked toward Tunis and Bizerte with three columns. One of these was halted before Mateur, the other one attacked Medjez el Bab and advanced to Djedeida, eventually raiding the airfield and destroying 20 German aircraft. On 28 November Kesselring arrived in Tunisia announcing that reinforcements were imminent and ordered the widening of the bridgehead. Nehring, facing a renewed Allied attack from Tebourba, adopted a 'defensive-offensive' attitude and, using the available armoured units (64 tanks, including two heavy Tigers), counterattacked the enemy positions at Tebourba on 1–3 December. Allied forces eventually withdrew while the German forces advanced to Medjez el Bab, where they were halted on 10 December and established a new defensive line. By then a 30km-wide (17-mile) bridgehead had been established from Bizerte to Pont du Fahs and the Allied advance was temporarily halted.

On 5 January 1943 Hitler ordered a reorganization of Kesselring's staff, splitting the functions of air and field commander. On 1 February Rommel's former chief of staff Siegfried Westphal transferred to Kesselring's field staff. On 26 January, following another order by Hitler, 5. Panzer Armee fell under Italian command (like Heeresgruppe Afrika, formed in February), while Kesselring reverted temporarily to the role of air commander and of liaison between the German and Italian commands. It was a difficult task; on 30 November 1942 the reinforced Luftflotte 2 had 1,646 (937 operational) aircraft, with a large number (551, 362 of which operational) of transport planes. Losses grew steadily in 1943; 282 in January, 206 in February, 308 in March and 572 in April, when transport units – now the main transport for Tunisia – fell victim to Allied fighters. On 5 April 13 Junkers Ju 52 were shot down, followed by another 18 on the 18th and 14 giant Messerschmitt Me 323s on the 22nd. At the end of the month a total of 76 Junkers Ju 52 had been lost. By March 1943 a depleted Luftflotte 2, with 1,086 aircraft of all kind (636 operational) faced some 4,547 Allied aircraft. On 12 June 1943 Generalfeldmarschall Wolfram von Richthofen arrived in Italy to take over command of Luftflotte 2. Kesselring was acting as Hitler's personal representative, conveying OKW's interests to the Italian commands, as the German units were still lacking field commands.

When Italian forces collapsed only three days after the Allied landing in Sicily on 10 July 1943, Hitler ordered XIV Panzer Korps to deploy to Sicily. The Germans more or less took control of the island from 16 July until its evacuation on 1–17 August. Following Mussolini's downfall on 25 July and the redeployment of German troops in northern Italy under Rommel's command, the OKW sanctioned the partition of Italy between Rommel's Heeresgruppe B (north of the line Pisa–Arezzo–Ancona) and Kesselring's OB Süd in the south. Three weeks later Italy surrendered, the Allies landed at Salerno, and the Italian campaign began.

Oberbefehlshaber Südwest

In August Kesselring deployed the HQ of LXXVI Panzer Korps to Calabria between 8 and 11 July, while on 15 August Generaloberst Heinrich von Vietinghoff was given command of the rebuilt AOK 10 that oversaw both XIV and LXXVI Panzer Korps from 22 July. On 3 September the Eighth Army crossed the Straits of Messina and started to advance north through Calabria. In spite of Italian assurances, it was clear that Italy's surrender was

A Sturmgeschütz III negotiating a river. The bulk of the German armour in Italy was made up of these self-propelled guns, that proved their effectiveness in that peculiar terrain. (Nik Cornish at Stavka)

only a matter of time. On 8 September 1943 Kesselring's forces were widely dispersed, with two divisions (3. Panzergrenadier, and 2. Fallschirmjäger under XI Flieger Korps) near Rome; three others under LXXVI Panzer Korps deployed in Calabria and Apulia (26. Panzer and 29. Panzergrenadier, 1. Fallschirmjäger in Apulia); and three others under XIV Panzer Korps in the Naples area (16. Panzer, 15. Panzergrenadier, Hermann Göring), plus the 90. Panzergrenadier-Division in Sardinia. An Allied landing in collaboration with Italian forces in the Rome area might have cut off the bulk of Kesselring's forces in the south, and General Westphal summed up the situation when he remarked that news of the Allied landing at Salerno on 8–9 September was welcomed with a 'sigh of relief'.

News of the Italian surrender on 8 September surprised no one. While 16. Panzer-Division immediately faced the Allied forces at Salerno, in Rome the situation was less critical. The king and many of his generals fled the city and a truce was declared on the 10th, which allowed 3. Panzergrenadier-Division to move south. Some 24,000 Italian soldiers disarmed in the city were set free to return to their homes. Determined to fight, Kesselring declared the area under his command 'war territory' on 11 September, while LXXVI Panzer Korps prepared to counterattack at Salerno. On 12 September German paratroopers rescued Mussolini.

German counterattacks against US Fifth Army units at Salerno started on 11 September, when the Hermann Göring and 15. Panzergrenadier divisions reached the area. The first heavy counterattacks were launched against US VI Corps on 13 September, followed by another against the British X Corps on 14–17 September. The Allies briefly considered withdrawal, but the strength of their naval gunfire beat back the German resistance and with the strengthening of Fifth Army at Salerno and the advance of the Eighth Army from Calabria and Apulia where Taranto had been seized on 9 September, Vietinghoff suggested putting a halt to the German counterattacks. Kesselring

Fatal Hours

On 8 September 1943, after a tip-off from the Italians, Kesselring's headquarters at the Hotel Tuscolum in Frascati was bombed. News of the Allied landing at Salerno arrived on the same day, when the Germans were already dealing with the Italian forces that, while surrendering to the Allies, were resisting every attempt from the German side to disarm them. However, within two days the two German divisions in Rome had brought the area under control and Italian forces in the city surrendered. Kesselring immediately released one division to Salerno, where the forces under the command of Generaloberst Heinrich von Vietinghoff started to counterattack the enemy beachhead on the 11th, only to launch a first, massive attack on the 13th. After five days of fighting, on 15 September, Kesselring (1) and Vietinghoff (2), along with Kesselring's chief of staff Siegfried Westphal (3), had a meeting to prepare a decisive counterattack for the following day. This would have been the last, however, and on 17 September the German forces started to withdraw.

Gebirgsjäger (mountain infantry) in shirtsleeve order manning a heavy machine-gun position under the cover of some bushes. These troops were amongst the best infantry units at Kesselring's disposal in Italy, along with the *Fallschirmjäger*. (Nik Cornish at Stavka)

agreed and German units started to pull back on 17 September to redeploy in the Salerno–Cerignola area on 18–19 September.

German units in Sardinia were evacuated to Corsica between 17 September and 4 October. On 19 September Fifth US and Eighth Armies established contact, while British units advanced to Bari, where the first Allied convoy arrived on 23 September. The situation while no longer considered critical, still remained difficult. On 20 September Kesselring ordered a staged withdrawal, a fighting retreat that would aim to hold the Allied advance and would enable his troops to defend the Reich as far away from Germany's borders as possible. Defences were established on three lines south of Rome, running west to east across the Italian peninsula along rivers and other natural obstacles. The Volturno Line was the most southerly, and ran from Termoli in the east, through the Apennines, to the Volturno River in the east. This was to be held until 15 October, then units would fall back to the Barbara Line 10–25km (6–15 miles) further north. The Bernhardt Line was established a further 20km or so north, but did not run right across the Italian Peninsula. It was a bulge on the western side, intended to delay the Allies before the Germans' strongest defences on the Gustav Line running on the Garigliano–Sangro rivers. The bulk of German forces started to deploy on the Volturno Line by 28 September and on 1 October the Allies entered Naples, establishing contact with the German line four days later. On 2 October British forces landed at Termoli, facing a German counterattack that was to last until 6 October. When the Fifth US Army crossed the Volturno on the night of 12–13 October heavy rain began to affect operations. Bridgeheads were established by the 15th, and on 16 October Vietinghoff authorized withdrawal to the Barbara Line.

Until the end of 1943, the war in Italy followed similar patterns, with the Germans gradually retreating north to prepared defensive lines. On 2–7 November Eighth Army crossed the Trigno River, while Fifth US Army advanced some 25 to 30km (15–18 miles) breaching the Barbara Line and approaching the Bernhardt Line, which XIV Panzer Korps had begun defending on 1 November. On 15 November Fifth Army commander, General Clark, ordered a two-week pause. The Italian campaign had already taken a definitive shape, and Kesselring had won another battle.

Kesselring's position in Italy was by no means secure, however. When Sicily fell, he was convinced that the Italians would continue to fight, and advised Hitler of this. Rommel was despatched to northern Italy and quickly reported that the Germans could not hold Italy without Italian support. Acting on this advice, Hitler ordered the withdrawal of Kesselring's forces from the south to join up with Rommel's troops in the north. Kesselring was horrified, however, believing that if southern Italy were abandoned, the Reich itself would be exposed to airborne attack by Allied bombers operating from Italian airfields. Feeling that he was being undermined by the refusal to place more troops under his command and following the arrival of Rommel in Italy, Kesselring offered his resignation on 14 August which was rejected by Hitler.

When the Italians surrendered on 8 September, Kesselring immediately secured Rome against an Allied invasion and demonstrated huge skill in slowing the Allied advance. On 4 October Hitler backed him up, and although he left the command situation unchanged, Rommel was to transfer two infantry divisions to Kesselring in exchange for the 90. Panzergrenadier-Division. The 16. Panzer-Division was sent to the Eastern Front and exchanged with the 5. Gebirgs-Division. Hitler remained greatly concerned about the possibility of an Allied landing behind German lines, and gradually accepted Kesselring's optimistic point of view, that the Allies could be stalled in a protracted series of defensive battles lasting six to nine months before reaching the northern Apennines.

Finally, on 6 November Hitler gave Kesselring overall command in Italy, as Oberbefehlshaber Südwest (Commander-in-Chief south-west) and commander of Heeresgruppe C, with complete control on all the forces in Italy. On 21 November 1943 Rommel left Italy for France.

Having won this battle, Kesselring faced more serious problems. The Bernhardt Line was still not complete, and OKW ordered Kesselring to reinforce it. Kesselring simply remarked that the line used natural features – the mountainous peaks of Monte Cassino – as strong defences and that German soldiers could defend it. On 6 November Vietinghoff went sick after harsh criticism from Kesselring, leaving his command to General der Panzertruppen Joachim Lemelsen until 28 December. The Adriatic front was threatened when the Eighth Army crossed the Sangro River on

Vietinghoff after his surrender to the Allies in May 1945. Along with Wolff and with the help of Dollmann, he negotiated a separate surrender with the American OSS representative in Switzerland. After the war neither he, nor Wolff nor Dollmann were tried by the Allies. (Count Ernesto G. Vitetti)

20 November, and between 27 November and 2 December the Gustav Line came under attack. On 30 November Kesselring asked for reinforcements to launch a counteroffensive on the Sangro, but on 1 December Hitler replied that such a counteroffensive would be useless and costly, and could only be undertaken if the weather prevented Allied air superiority.

On 6–8 December Fifth US Army attacked the Bernhardt Line, and although German units in San Pietro held out until the 17th, by the end of the year Allied forces had the Gustav Line in their sights. On 8–20 December Eighth Army battled for the Moro River line, eventually reaching Ortona on the 27th shortly before General Montgomery handed over command to General Leese on the 30th. Once more Kesselring faced a moment of crisis, lacking reserves and reinforcements, although inclement weather and the exhaustion of Allied soldiers worked in his favour. On 20 December OKW ordered him to prepare plans in case of an Allied landing on the Italian coast. On 29 December Hitler expressed his anxiety about a possible Allied landing, but Kesselring's optimism reassured him.

General der Panzertruppen Joachim Lemelsen, commander of AOK 14 from June to October 1944 and from February to May 1945, who also led AOK 10 from October 1944 while Kesselring was ill. (Count Ernesto G. Vitetti)

Anzio and Cassino

Despite the lack of reserves, Kesselring made good use of his forces. He used simple tactics, rotating units (down to battalion level) to and from the front, often switching them to different sectors to rest and recover while protecting the coasts. The possibility of an Allied landing behind the front was a major concern for the Germans. Kesselring and his staff devised a plan to deal with this eventuality based on the redeployment of units within the Italian front and on using reinforcements from Germany and German-occupied territories (a total of four divisions, along with the equivalent of two more).

The first plan confronted a major landing, on the Tyrrhenian coast (*Marder 1*) and one on the Adriatic coast (*Marder 2*). On 12 January 1944

1. On 11 and 12 November the Tunis and Bizerte bridgeheads are established under command of Oberst Harlinghausen (who formed a *Kampfgruppe* with three coys of a replacement battalion, detachments of Fallschirmjäger-Regiment 5, 14. Kompanie of Panzergrenadier-Regiment 104 and a Flak battery) and Oberst Lederer (forming a *Kampfgruppe* with one coy from the replacement battalion, 4. Kompanie of Panzer-Abteilung 190, 4./Artillerie-Regiment 2 and a battery from Artillerie-Regiment 190); on 14 November XC Corps is formed to control both bridgeheads, becoming 5. Panzerarmee on 9 December.

1. 8–9 September 1943, Allied landing at Salerno.
2. German counterattacks, 11–17 September.
3. Allied advances after link-up with the Eighth Army on

16 September, advancing from the south across the Messina strait, and the beginning of Kesselring's staged withdrawal north.

4. Allied advances in the north: 78th British Division first to advance after landing at Bari on 22–23 September, followed at first by British 5th Division, Canadian 1st Division assembling at Potenza then at Foggia (from the Messina strait), and eventually by 8th Indian Division and 2nd New Zealand Division;
5. On 2 October British Commandos seize Termoli.
6. On 12 October the Fifth US Army crosses the Volturno line and starts advancing north, with the British X Corps on the left flank.
7. Advance of US VI Corps from 12 October.
8. Advance of British XIII Corps (Eighth Army) towards Isernia.
9. Advance of British V Corps along the northern coast.

Staged withdrawal in Italy, September–November 1943

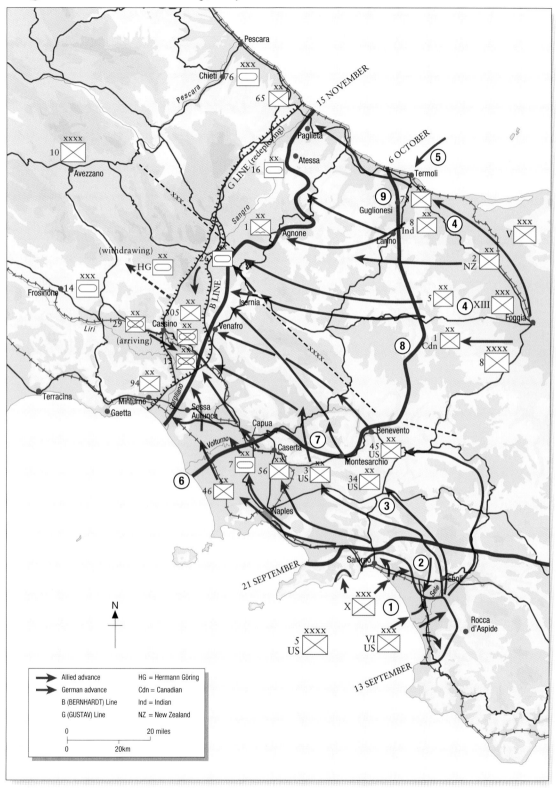

Pescara

Chieti • 76 [XXX]

65 [XX]

15 NOVEMBER

G LINE (redeploying)

Paglieta

Atessa

6 OCTOBER

Termoli ⑤

16 [XX]

10 [XXXX]

Avezzano

Sangro

⑨ 78 [XX]

Guglionesi

8 Ind [XX] ④

V [XXX]

XXX

1 [XX]

Agnone

Larino

2 NZ [XX]

(withdrawing)

HG [XX]

26 [XX]

B LINE

Isernia

5 [XX]

④ XIII [XXX]

Frosinone • 14 [XXX]

305 [XX]

Venafro

8 ⑧

Foggia

29 [XX] Cassino

Liri

[XX]

(arriving)

15 [XX]

xxxx

1 Cdn [XX]

8 [XXXX]

94 [XX]

Garigliano

Terracina

Minturno

Gaetta

Sessa Aurunca

Capua

Benevento

45 US [XX]

Caserta

Montesarchio

Volturno

7 [XX]

56 [XX]

3 US [XX]

34 US [XX]

③

⑥

46 [XX]

Naples

21 SEPTEMBER

Salerno

②

Eboli

Sele

X [XXX] ①

Rocca d'Aspide

N

5 US [XXXX]

VI US [XXX]

13 SEPTEMBER

Allied advance   HG = Hermann Göring
German advance   Cdn = Canadian
B (BERNHARDT) Line   Ind = Indian
G (GUSTAV) Line   NZ = New Zealand

0   20 miles
0   20km

39

a second, more detailed plan was drawn up to deal with different possibilities, such as landings in the area of Rome (codenamed *Richard*), Leghorn (*Ludwig*), Genoa (*Gustav*), the Rimini–Venice coast (*Victor*), and in Istria (Ida). Since the forces available to guard the coastline were scarce, they were mainly intended to check the enemy beachheads until reinforcements made a major counterattack possible.

By mid-January 1944 the availability of troops was Kesselring's greatest concern. Eight divisions were deployed at the front, with 3. Panzergrenadier moving to the Adriatic sector to relieve 26. Panzer, and the 71. Infanterie on its way from the north to Cassino, where it was expected to arrive on 17 January. Elements of the Hermann Göring Division were deployed at the front or in the rear area of XIV Panzer Korps, leaving AOK 10 with only two reserve units deployed near Rome: 29 and 90. Panzergrenadier-Division. The 4. Fallschirmjäger-Division was forming north of the city. Both the Hermann Göring and 90. Panzergrenadier divisions were scheduled for redeployment from Italy, to be replaced by the 114. Jäger (light infantry) from Yugoslavia and the 371. Infanterie divisions, the latter eventually sent to the Eastern Front.

Even in the north, where AOK 14 had replaced Rommel's Heeresgruppe B in November 1943, units were scarce, with four of the seven available divisions still forming. Intelligence reports on 12 and 14 January suggested that an enemy landing in Italy was likely, but this was soon regarded as less so. The French Expeditionary Corps' attack against the Gustav Line on 11 January was the first sign of a major offensive, followed on the 17th by British X Corps' attack on the lower Garigliano River. The breakthrough that occurred in this sector spread havoc amongst German commanders. Vietinghoff reported that no reserves were available and on the 18th Kesselring decided to commit the only two available reserves, the 29. and 90. Panzergrenadier divisions. This left the whole Rome area without any significant units, and Kesselring explained in his memoirs that he did not expect a major landing in the region.

Fallschirmjäger manning a 50mm PaK 38 anti-tank gun. Note the rather odd mixture of uniforms, with the men on the left wearing jump smocks, while the man in the foreground wears a camouflage quarter and an army helmet. (Filippo Cappellano)

Testing the new weapon first hand. Kesselring (wearing tropical uniform) sits behind the commander's cupola of a Sturmgeschütz IV self-propelled gun during firing exercises in Italy. (Author's collection)

In the meantime, he hoped that once the situation had been restored, those two divisions could quickly be deployed elsewhere.

On 22 January US VI Corps landed at Anzio, taking the few German defenders completely by surprise, while two days before the US 36th Division's attempts to cross the Rapido River marked the beginning of a new phase of the offensive against the Gustav Line, that reached its climax with US II Corps' attack against Cassino from 24 January. But the Anzio landing was the major threat, and the reaction was prompt. Kesselring's command issued the codeword *Richard* at 0600hrs on 22 January and gave orders to prepare for the redeployment of 29. and 3. Panzergrenadier divisions, while 26. Panzer-Division was ordered to Anzio at full speed. The same day, Kesselring instructed the German commander of Rome to take over command of the area and to prepare a defensive line using every available unit, while 4. Fallschirmjäger-Division was given orders to move to Rome at once, along with the HQ of I Fallschirm Korps (formed from XI Flieger Korps). On 23 January Kesselring visited the front at Anzio, and concluded that even though the landing enabled the Allies to seize valuable territory, the Allied commanders were not following up their advantage. This impression was confirmed by the first patrols, who reported that the enemy was more interested in securing the beachhead than advancing inland. On 23–24 January the HQs and advanced elements of the 3. Panzergrenadier and the Hermann Göring divisions arrived at Anzio, followed by the HQ of I Fallschirm Korps. The German build-up had started.

On 25 January the HQ of AOK 14 took over command at Anzio where elements of eight German divisions were deployed against the US VI Corps. The Germans rushed to beat back the Allies before they broke out from the beachhead, but reinforcements were slow to arrive and Kesselring was forced to delay until 1 February. On 29 January US VI Corps attacked from the beachhead toward Campoleone station with the British 1st Division and the US 1st Armored, while the US 3rd Division attacked toward Cisterna.

A portrait of Generalfeldmarschall Wolfram von Richthofen, who took over command of Luftflotte 2 from Kesselring on 26 June 1943 and led it until it was disbanded on 27 September 1944. He died of cancer on 12 July 1945. (Count Ernesto G. Vitetti)

Neither objective was seized, and on 31 January the attack was called off. Early in February the German situation was still critical, but steadily improving. On 24 January the French attack north of Cassino came to a halt, only to be revived 25 January–3 February by the attack on Colle Belvedere. In February the attacks of the British X and of the US II Corps came to a halt respectively on 9 and 12 February, and the first attack by the New Zealand Corps against the city and the hill of Cassino on 15–18 February marked the beginning of a new phase of the battle, as the Allies attempted to break through the most stubborn bastion of the German defence in Italy. Meanwhile, by 1 February some 95,000 Germans, from seven different divisions, were deployed at Anzio and two days later the first German counterattack was launched. By 5 February Allied forces had been pushed back some 3km (2 miles) to Aprilia, while the attacks that followed on 8–11 February pushed the Allied forces further back, both at Aprilia and at Cisterna. On 16 February, now with eight divisions at their disposal (four infantry, one Panzer, two *Panzergrenadier*, one *Fallschirmjäger*), the German counteroffensive began in earnest. The balance of forces, the decision to attack along the main road from Aprilia to Anzio, and poor weather that made off-road movements difficult, ended the counteroffensive just 4km (2.5 miles) from its starting point on 19 February. On 29 February a second counteroffensive was launched and was met with a storm of artillery fire from both land and sea. It ground to a halt on 2 March without any major achievement.

After the failure of the German counteroffensives at Anzio and the second (according to German numbering) battle of Cassino fought on 15–23 March, both sides paused for two months. Although there was a stalemate, Kesselring knew that time was running out.

The final campaign

By May 1944 the German situation in Italy had worsened, while the Allies strengthened their position. By mid-month only five German divisions were facing the Anzio beachhead (three infantry, one *Fallschirmjäger* and one

1. 71. Infanterie-Division moves south to relieve the Hermann Göring Division, expected in the Liri Valley area 17 January.
2. 3. Panzergrenadier-Division moves to the LXXVI Panzer Korps area, but then retraces its steps and is committed at Cassino on 20 January.
3. Elements of the Hermann Göring Division committed to Cassino on 18 January.
4. 29. Panzergrenadier-Division moves to Cassino on 19 January.
5. 90. Panzergrenadier-Division moves to Cassino on 21 January.

6. 5th Canadian Armoured committed to Sangro area in late January.
7. 4th Indian Division relieves the US 34th Division in early February.

A. British X Corps attack on the Garigliano, 17 January.
B. US II Corps attempts to cross the Rapido, 20 January.
C. US VI Corps lands at Anzio, 22 January.
D. French Expeditionary Corps attacks at Monte Cairo, 24 January.

First Battle of Cassino and Anzio, 18–22 January 1944

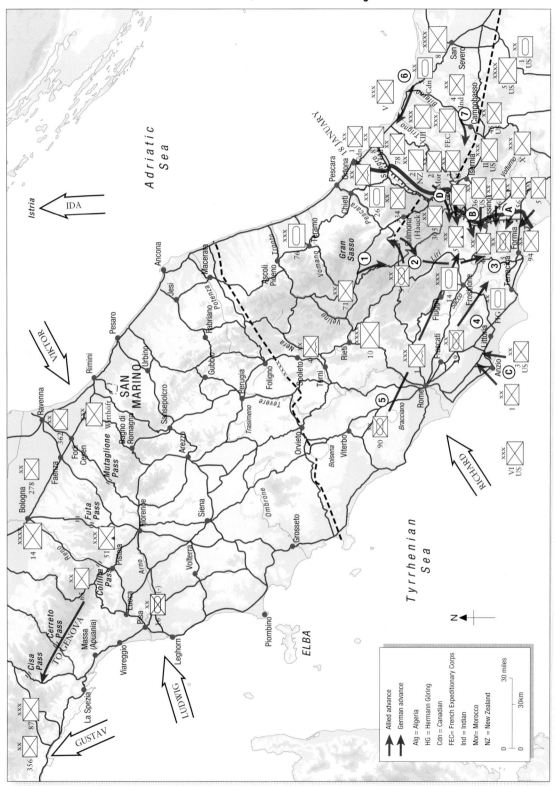

Generalleutnant Richard Heidrich, commander of 1. Fallschirmjäger-Division during the Cassino battles, describes the situation to Kesselring, who observes the maps while seated at the table. (Count Ernesto G. Vitetti)

Panzergrenadier) while another eight divisions, and three infantry divisions on the Adriatic, were deployed at Cassino (four infantry, one mountain, two *Panzergrenadier*, one *Fallschirmjäger*). The only available reserves were the two divisions at the disposal of AOK 14 (92. Infanterie, 29. Panzergrenadier) and the two Panzer divisions under direct command of Kesselring's HQ (26. Panzer, and Hermann Göring). Lacking detailed intelligence on the Allied forces or their intentions, Kesselring's command could not decide whether they were about to launch another major offensive or another landing in Italy. With no expectations of any reinforcement from outside the area, Kesselring's strategy was to adapt to the situation. With a lack of manpower, there were no deep defences and, at Anzio in particular, he relied on the area's marshy terrain for protection. Kesselring initiated 'staged withdrawal' tactics, and defensive lines (mostly on paper) were established north of Cassino and Anzio ('C' line), south of Rome, while the construction of the Gothic Line in the northern Apennines continued. Shortly after the Allied 'Diadem' offensive started on 11 May, it was clear that it could not be contained. By 13 May Kesselring authorized withdrawal from the Gustav Line in the Cassino area and on the 16th the whole Cassino front was in movement. On 18 May Kesselring committed the 26. Panzer-Division in the northern area of the battle, but two days later the Fifth US Army broke through in the south and started to advance along the coast.

On 23 May US VI Corps attacked from the Anzio beachhead, soon breaking through toward Cisterna, and a counterattack by the Hermann Göring Division planned for the 26th could not be launched. The link-up on the same

Fallschirmjäger manning an anti-tank gun position in an Italian town. Although 1. Fallschirmjäger-Division is best known for its defence of Cassino, it fought a skilled and brave rearguard action on the Adriatic coast in 1943–44 that ended with the battle of Ortona. (Piero Crociani)

A view of Cassino and 'hangman hill' at the end of the battle, or rather a view of what was left of them given the extent of destruction caused by the air and artillery bombardments. (Piero Crociani)

day between the US VI and II Corps completely altered the situation from the German point of view, and even Hitler had to agree that a withdrawal north was necessary. General Clark's decision to alter the advance of most of the US VI Corps, to the north from the west where they threatened the rear lines of AOK 10, greatly eased the German situation and by 30 May redeployment on the 'C' line was started. The Allied breakthrough on the AOK 14 front on 27–28 May, and the failure of the German counterattacks marked the end of the battle, however. While Hitler ordered every possible reinforcement to Italy, on 2 June Kesselring asked for authorization to retreat north of Rome. Withdrawal started the following day, and on 4 June Fifth US Army entered Rome, ending the nine-month campaign. Kesselring sacked Generaloberst Eberhard von Mackensen, the commander of AOK 14, the same day and replaced him with General Lemelsen.

After the fall of Rome and the landings in Normandy on 6 June 1944, the Italian campaign entered a new phase; Kesselring's forces, already depleted, were further reduced as troops were sent to other fronts. The staged

A meeting between Kesselring and Graziani, the commander-in-chief of Mussolini's armed forces in 1943–45, during a less formal occasion, when all wear tropical uniforms. To the right is Oberst Karl-Heinrich Graf von Klinckowstroem, Kesselring's Ia (operations officer) from August to December 1943. (Andrea Molinari)

withdrawal became a race between Kesselring, who was trying to buy time while the Gothic Line was completed, and the Allies, who were trying to maximize their gains before diverting forces for the landing in southern France. By 20 June the Allied advance had reached the Trasimene Line, some 120km (75 miles) north of Rome. Even though the pace of advance slowed down, by the end of July the Allies approached the Arno Line and Florence, covering almost 200km (125 miles) in just six weeks. This was especially fast when compared to the 120km (75 miles) advanced from Salerno to Cassino in almost four months. By mid-July the German situation in Italy was critical again, with AOK 10 having only 12 divisions, half of them down to the size of a *Kampfgruppe*, and AOK 14 having only eight, two of *Kampfgruppe* size. Taking advantage of the terrain, the Germans held the Arno Line from 18 July to 15 August. Florence was evacuated by German troops on 10 August in an effort to prevent major damage to the historic city. The Allied landing in southern France on 15 August also marked a change of direction, with the

Cassino 1944

The three battles (four according to Allied numbering) fought at Cassino between January and May 1944 are part of the epic of warfare. The image of the ruined Benedictine monastery atop the hill of Monte Cassino, with soldiers fighting bitterly for every step, is a strong one. Fighting amongst rubble, the *Fallschirmjäger* were able to turn the situation to their advantage using the stone-built cellars as shelters and seeking protection from the remains of buildings that could no longer burn or collapse under fire. This way they could hide from enemy artillery fire, and surface after the advancing enemy had exhausted every weapon in their arsenal; they are shown here equipped with a, MG42 machine gun and an 81mm medium mortar.

Observing the developments at the Anzio beachhead first-hand; Kesselring (right, with binoculars), General der Flieger Maximilian Ritter von Pohl (commander of the German land-based Luftwaffe organization) and Generalfeldmarschall Wolfram von Richthofen, commander of Luftflotte 2. (Author's collection)

Allied efforts in Italy now being re-directed to the Adriatic coast, where the flatter plains seemed more suited for a major offensive.

The temporary cessation had mixed effects on the German side: two *Panzergrenadier* divisions were redeployed from Italy to France, while Kesselring asked permission to withdraw back to the advanced positions of the Gothic (now officially Green) Line and pull three divisions out of the line and put them in reserve. AOK 10 started its actual redeployment on 22 August, followed by AOK 14 at the end of the month, and on the 29th Hitler authorized further withdrawal to the main Gothic Line positions. In spite of works that had lasted for several months, the Gothic Line soon revealed many weaknesses. It was still not ready, many areas were still incomplete, with exposed strongholds facing the enemy. Kesselring's staff immediately started to look for suitable positions to build a 'Gothic Line 2', and this put further strain on Kesselring's troops, who were mostly depleted and lacking supplies and weapons. At the end of August there were 15 divisions on the line, mostly infantry (12), along with the 16. SS-Panzergrenadier-Division 'Reichsführer SS' and two *Fallschirmjäger* divisions. 29. Panzergrenadier-Division was the only reserve, while a further 12 German divisions were deployed along the coasts or further inland, ready to be deployed to the front if necessary (these included 26. Panzer and 90. Panzergrenadier divisions, eight infantry divisions of various quality and two mountain divisions).

The first phase of the battle for the Gothic Line (Operation *Olive*) started on 25 August with Eighth Army's attack against the German positions on the Metauro River, south of Pesaro. They surprised the withdrawing Germans and after three days of fighting AOK 10 units withdrew to the Green Line running along the Foglia River. The attack against the Gothic Line proper started on 30 August and soon turned into a drama for the Germans. By 3 September Canadian I and British V Corps broke through the German line, swarming onto the plain, and eventually forcing Kesselring to commit his reserves and bring six divisions into the line. The Gothic Line 2 was no stronger than the old one, but the Eighth Army offensive quickly

Fallschirmjäger Feldgendarme (military police) check their maps (note how they wear the standard army gorget rather than the Luftwaffe one). Control of the ground was essential in Italy, to secure areas from the partisans' threat and to maintain supply routes. (Count Ernesto G. Vitetti)

ran into trouble. The battle fought between 3 and 6 September at Coriano Ridge checked the Allied offensive for the first time, as did the battle for Gemmano Ridge on 7–12 September. A new phase of the offensive began on 13 September and on the following day Eighth Army troops had advanced beyond both ridges, while on the central Apennines US II and British XIII Corps attacked the German positions astride the mountain road leading from Florence to Bologna.

Once more the terrain and the weather were critical factors for Kesselring's defence. Having captured the il Giogo and Futa passes, on 18 September the Fifth Army stopped the first phase of its offensive, while on the Adriatic side, the seizure of Rimini on 21 September by the Eighth Army seemed to open the gateway to the Romagna plain. But stubborn German resistance, heavy rains that turned roads into mud and flooded streams made even this phase extremely hard, with the Eighth Army advancing only 50km (31 miles) in 26 days. On 23 September the Eighth Army's new offensive started the 'battle of the rivers', fought on a stretch of land some 40km (25 miles) deep from Rimini to Ravenna. However, it soon proved to be simply a repetition of the old 'just another hill' (with the variation 'just another river') tune, all too familiar to those who had been fighting in Italy since September 1943. On 24 September Fifth Army started a new phase of its offensive, that by 1 October had reached the mountain peaks in front of Imola and the Bologna plain.

By mid-October most of the available units in Italy – 19 divisions out of 28 – were deployed at the front, with only two divisions held in reserve and five second-rate divisions along the coasts. On 23 October, Kesselring's car collided with a towed artillery piece and the injuries he suffered practically put an end to his command in Italy. The fighting, however, lasted until January 1945, when another pause was the prelude to the final Allied offensive.

Kesselring as a witness
during the Nuremberg
trials, March 1946.
(Private collection)

Kesselring's absence brought no real change to the situation on the German side, with Vietinghoff taking over command and fighting the battle as Kesselring would have done. Kesselring returned to Italy between January and March, before being given command in the West on 9 March, two days after the capture of the Remagen Bridge on the Rhine. There was little, if anything, he could do to prevent the Allied advance into Germany, but there was still something he could do before the war ended. On 28 April 1945 he was appointed Oberbefehlshaber Süd, in command of the entire southern sector, including southern Germany, Italy and the Balkans. On 29 April, concluding negotiations begun in March between German representatives and the chief of the Office of Strategic Services in Switzerland, Vietinghoff's own representatives signed the surrender of the German forces in Italy, effective on 2 May. Once Kesselring heard this news, he relieved Vietinghoff of his command and tried to have him arrested, only to face the final German surrender in Italy. Six days later it was his turn to surrender to the Allies.

1. Start of Operation *Diadem*, 11 May.
2. US VI Corps attacks from the Anzio bridgehead, 22 January.
3. Link up between US VI and II Corps, 25 May.
4. Fifth US Army enters Rome, 4 June.
5. US IV Corps relieves US VI Corps, 11 June.
6. Landing at Elba and seizure by French troops, 19 June. Between late July and early August the Allied drive to northern Italy reached its culmination point; on 18 July Ancona was seized by the Eighth Army, and on the 18th Leghorn was seized by the Fifth US Army. On 23 July Fifth US Army was on the Arno and on 5 August the Allied forces entered Florence. At this point the Germans started to shift back north towards the defences of the Gothic Line while the Allied forces start their build-up to launch the final attack.
7. Operation *Olive*, the attack against the Gothic Line, starts on 25 August; on the 30th the Gothic Line is breached at Pesaro. This is the start of the battle of the Gothic Line and by November 1944 the Eighth Army is in the Po Valley without any breakthrough being achieved.
8. Fifth US Army first attacks on Gothic Line north of Florence, 10–18 September. Although the line is broken through and the Fifth US Army offensive manages to reach northern slopes of the Apennines facing Bologna by the end of October, it too cannot achieve any breakthrough.

Staged withdrawal in Central Italy, May–November 1944

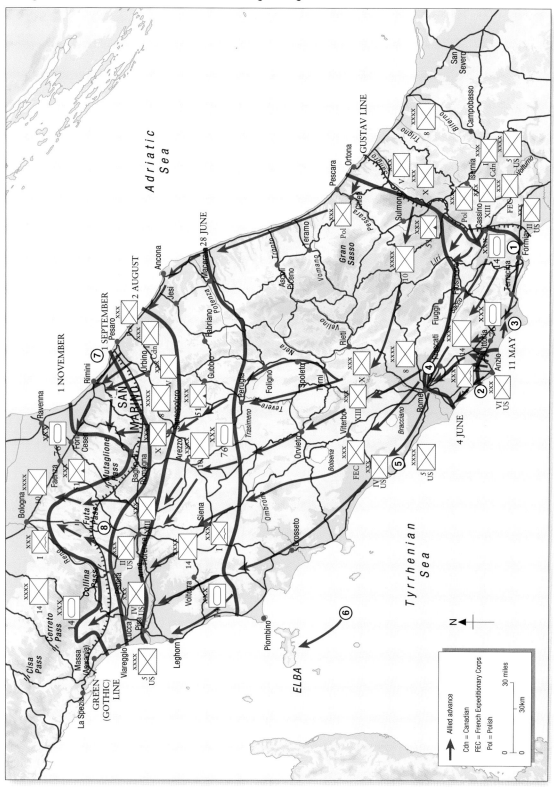

OPPOSING COMMANDERS

Air Chief Marshal Sir Hugh Dowding with HM King George VI. (Count Ernesto G. Vitetti)

Air Chief Marshal Sir Hugh Dowding

Born in Scotland in 1882, Dowding was an artillery officer who became a pilot in 1913 and joined the Royal Flying Corps during World War I. A squadron commander in 1915, he ended the war as a brigadier-general. He was in charge of research and development in the RAF, and was therefore involved in the development of Radio Direction Finders (later known as radar). In 1936 he was at the head of Fighter Command, spending the following years preparing against the German threat. Due to retire in 1938, he was asked to remain in his job and developed the British defence system based on radar, communication and control, and the fighter units. During the campaign in Norway Dowding opposed the dispersion of the fighters, and did so again during the battle of France much to Churchill's regret (those fighters had been promised to the French). In July–August 1940 Dowding's Fighter Command was the only force to oppose the Germans, after the victories in Europe. Although the battle was actually fought by individual Fighter Groups, the overall strategy (and in particular the handling of pilots and aircraft) was always in Dowding's hands. His lack of people skills led, however, to clashes between his commanders, notably on the 'big wing' strategy, which he did not handle well. On 24 November 1940 he left Fighter Command, and after a period spent in the USA for the Ministry of Aircraft Production, he retired in July 1942. He died in 1970.

Field Marshal Sir Harold Alexander. (Count Ernesto G. Vitetti)

Field Marshal Sir Harold Alexander

Born 1891, he served with distinction during World War I and by 1937 became the youngest general in the British Army. During World War II he took over command of the British Expeditionary Force during the evacuation of Dunkirk, then, having commanded the British Army forces in the south of England, in the south of England, was sent to Burma early in 1942. Promoted to full general in April, he was recalled in July to be given command of First Army scheduled to take part in scheduled to take part in the French North Africa landing. However, prior to this, Churchill appointed him to the position of Commander-in-Chief, Middle East Command, in August, with overall responsibility for Montgomery's successful campaign. In January 1943 Alexander became General Dwight Eisenhower's deputy and assumed command of the newly formed 18th Army Group on 20 February, leading the last phase of the Tunisian campaign. As commander of the 15th Army Group he also commanded the Allied forces in Italy, which he led during the invasion of Sicily and then during the Italian campaign from Salerno to the Gothic Line. On 27 November 1944 he became Allied Supreme Commander in the Mediterranean, and was promoted to Field Marshal. A markedly different character to Kesselring, he lacked his opponent's technical knowledge and was slower in his reactions. It was Alexander, amongst others, who openly opposed the death penalty for Kesselring.

General Mark W. Clark with General Lucian K. Truscott. (Count Ernesto G. Vitetti)

General Mark W. Clark

Born in 1896, Clark served in France during World War I. In June 1942 he took over command of US II Corps, became Eisenhower's deputy and led negotiations with the Vichy forces in French North Africa. Success earned him promotion and in November 1942 he became the youngest lieutenant general in the US Army. In January 1943, he took over command of the newly formed Fifth US Army, part of Alexander's 15th Army Group. Clark was in command of the Salerno landings and in the subsequent advance along the Italian peninsula, entering Naples but without achieving the decisive breakthrough that would have opened up the road to Rome. He was one of the minds behind Operation *Shingle*, the landing at Anzio, and organized the attack of II Corps across the Rapido, that ended in failure and the loss of 2,100 dead in one day. He was criticized for his handling of this operation even after the war ended. During Operation *Diadem* Clark's decision to switch the axis of US VI Corps' advance from Anzio beachhead from the west to the north, toward Rome, was controversial, but on 4 June 1944 he entered the eternal city. In December 1944 he replaced Alexander at the head of 15th Army Group, and in March 1945 he rose to the rank of a four star general. After the war he was in command of the Allied forces in Austria, then led a military academy in the United States. A good organizer, trainer and planner, and with friends in high places, he lacked the true command and leadership skills of a field general. He died in 1984.

INSIDE THE MIND

Kesselring used to describe himself as a 'self-made man', which was certainly true given his remarkable achievements during World War I and in the inter-war years. He certainly did not lack self-confidence, and he possessed all the qualities of a first-class staff officer, such as organizational skills,

Fallschirmjäger check a street in Rome, 10 September 1943. Thanks to the swift action of 2. Fallschirmjäger-Division, which penetrated the city with six battalions in just two days, the Italian resistance was broken down quickly. (Count Ernesto G. Vitetti)

technical knowledge and a strong will. It is hard to say to what extent being transferred to the Luftwaffe influenced him, but the period he spent first on the Luftwaffe staff, and then as an air commander, is revealing. One thing ought to be stressed: from the very beginning, the *Führerprinzip* ('leader principle') ruled the Luftwaffe: orders were given from the top down and chiefs were responsible for implementing them. In effect, the nature of air warfare meant that commanders could not closely control their subordinates, who carried out the 'mission orders' principle to implement their orders. Several Luftflotte commanders exercised iron control, among them Deßloch, Löhr, Keller and Sperrle. Kesselring, like his colleagues, issued guidelines or directives, and the details were worked out by subordinates and put into effect by air unit commanders. This is certainly one of the reasons that Kesselring made frequent visits to local commands and units, since these were his main sources of information and enabled him to evaluate situations at first hand.

This was one of Kesselring's main limitations: his judgement was too often impaired by his optimism. However, this is balanced by the fact that Luftwaffe intelligence produced notoriously inflated figures about the destruction of enemy aircraft, which meant that judgements made by German air commanders were inaccurate during both the campaigns in Western Europe of May–June 1940 and the Battle of Britain. Kesselring was undoubtedly an optimist, but he was working with poor intelligence data.

In the early stages of the Italian campaign, however, Kesselring's optimism was rooted in reality and he produced a better assessment of the situation than Rommel. Rommel's advice to withdraw north to defend Italy on the northern Apennines was both premature and unrealistic, because he would have surrendered most of the Italian Peninsula to the Allies without a fight. On the other hand, Kesselring's view of the situation often matched the views of his superiors, notably Hitler. This is certainly what happened when Kesselring abruptly changed his opinion about the decision to invade Egypt and to sacrifice the planned assault on Malta, which he initially regarded as the strategic cornerstone of the war in the Mediterranean. Rommel criticized Kesselring's overly optimistic opinions in a letter written to his wife on 5 January 1943, from Tunisia, in which he said that Kesselring blamed him for the lack of success on the battlefield.

Kesselring's attitude toward his subordinates, his fellow commanders and his own superiors also provides an insight into his command and leadership qualities. Kesselring's inclination to please his superiors, above all Hitler and Göring, is writ large throughout his career as an air commander. In a post-war account of the air war in the West, written for the US Air Force by Kesselring's chief of staff, the author clearly believes that Kesselring should have prevented any interference from Hitler or Göring during the planning stage of the airborne assault on Holland. Hitler exercised great influence on Kesselring, who claimed that from 1942 almost every decision depended on him. Kesselring had an open attitude toward National Socialism, but it is interesting that he strongly resisted attempts to impose ideological doctrines on the Luftwaffe.

In spite of his affability and diplomatic attitude (when dealing with the Italians), Kesselring could be difficult to deal with, particularly when communicating with his peers. This was certainly the case with Rommel, a man five years younger than him, who lacked any staff experience but was already a rising star and one of Hitler's favourites when Kesselring arrived in the Mediterranean. Kesselring did not spare his censure of Rommel, particularly after the war ended and Rommel was dead. After becoming Oberbefehlshaber Süd, Kesselring openly criticized the lack of secure lines of communication and supply across the Mediterranean that greatly hampered the operations in North Africa.

As an experienced general staff officer, Kesselring compared the situation in the Mediterranean and in North Africa to the one he had faced while commanding Luftflotte 2 on the Eastern Front in 1941. He was rightly proud that his air fleet was always adequately supplied in Russia, thanks to the effective relationship between the quartermaster and operation officers. He observed that Rommel's military advances were often conducted at the expense of his troops, as the logistical side struggled to keep pace and German soldiers endured difficult battlefield conditions. As early as May 1942 Kesselring argued that the commander of Panzerarmee Afrika should be replaced, simply because of Rommel's unconventional style of command. The timing was certainly wrong, but in the long run Kesselring demonstrated steadier nerves and a very different style of command and leadership qualities to the 'Desert Fox'.

When under great pressure during the Italian campaign, however, Kesselring sometimes acted harshly. He clashed with Vietinghoff, who took sick leave after he criticized him. However, Vietinghoff seems to have been highly strung, because in 1941, while commanding XXXXVI Armee Korps on the Eastern Front, he complained directly to the chief of the OKW, Generalfeldmarschall Keitel, because he felt he had been passed over for promotion. After a heated exchange of letters, Vietinghoff asked to be relieved of his command and to be transferred to the West, which happened in 1942 after a period in the officers' reserve. Kesselring's decision to sack Mackensen and to replace him at the head of AOK 14 on 4 June 1944 may have seemed tough, but it also demonstrates an incisive management style.

One of the most interesting aspects of Kesselring's career is how the opposing sides regard his handling of the Italian campaign very differently. The Allies regarded him as a master strategist, who actually made the difference during the campaign. Kesselring undoubtedly made a number of mistakes, such as the proposal to start a counteroffensive against the Eighth Army at Ortona, when he was already faced with a double offensive at

Cassino and Anzio in January 1944. It is also interesting that when Vietinghoff took over command in late October 1944, he fought the battles on the Gothic Line as Kesselring would have done. Yet from the very beginning, Kesselring had a grasp of the strategic realities of the Italian campaign, which he understood much better than Rommel ever did. In spite of Allied air superiority and particularly vulnerable lines of communication, Kesselring was always able to keep his troops supplied and to move them from one sector of the front to another, even when there was practically nothing left of his Luftflotte 2.

Ironically, the Germans were more vocal in their condemnation of Kesselring's command and leadership. In his post-war accounts written for the US Army, Vietinghoff largely criticized Kesselring and his style of command. He was, in Vietinghoff's words, a strong personality, a first-class organizer and a charming person, who made his headquarters a very welcoming place. On the other hand, he was excessively close to Hitler, to whom he remained loyal until the very end, and for this reason he was an advocate of static, rigid defence. Vietinghoff, a former Panzer troop commander, claims that he himself advocated a mobile defence that would have offered the same resistance against the Allied advance but with fewer sacrifices. Although Vietinghoff overplayed his role, his remarks are interesting. In his opinion the Allies overestimated German capabilities, which led to two basic mistakes: first, the decision to land in areas too close to their own lines (within range of their air fields), and second, the decision to focus on Cassino when an advance along the Adriatic coast would have been a better option, at least geographically.

These observations are worth considering. In spite of the eventual failure at Anzio and the troubled situation at Salerno, it is true that a landing further inland might have been strategically decisive both in 1943 and in 1944. In the first case it was quite clear that an Allied landing in the Rome area might have had disastrous consequences for the Germans; in the second, one should focus on Kesselring's reaction plans to fully understand the situation. The fact that he devised plans to face an Allied landing all along the northern part of the Italian Peninsula shows that the Germans feared this eventuality. In fact, from the German side, the Allied landing at Anzio, with relatively few forces and away from major harbours, was almost a side-show, since it was too far from the frontline and thus posed very little threat to the German defences. It was only thanks to the relatively slow German build-up and to the equally fast Allied one that the Germans were not able to achieve real superiority on the battlefield and throw the enemy back into the sea. In conclusion, Vietinghoff's remark about the suitability of the Adriatic coast as the real breakthrough area for the Allied offensive shows that Kesselring's 'absurd' idea of a counteroffensive was at least understandable. For he certainly realized the danger of Eighth Army's advance in the area.

Kesselring's personality, as well as his command and leadership skills, was fairly complex. He was much more than either one of the polarized views that emerged after 1945, as either a great commander, or on the other side of the coin, a war criminal.

WHEN WAR IS DONE

The extent and the complexity of the partisan (and anti-partisan) war in Italy in 1943–45 cannot be dealt with in detail in this context, but a brief summary is necessary to understand Kesselring's post-war trial. In 1947, he was accused of war crimes, specifically relating to the Ardeatine Cave massacre of 1944.

Following the Italian surrender in September 1943, ex-members of the armed forces provided the bulk of the Italian resistance movement against German forces. Whether a deliberate choice or the consequence of the situation, Kesselring's decision to disarm Italian soldiers and allow them to go home meant that Italian resistance was mainly focused in north-west Italy, in the area under Rommel's control. Rommel followed a policy of deporting Italian troops or forcing them to fight in German units and this produced great resentment. In addition, on the north-eastern border, a vicious partisan war was being fought by Yugoslav partisans.

Things were to change in the winter and spring of 1943–44, when the Italian partisan movement increased both in numbers and intensity. Figures grew from 4,000–5,000 partisans in October 1943, to about 13,000 in February–March 1944, and were as high as 20,000–30,000 including followers and sympathizers. The Italian partisans were broken down into different groups, working either on the political or the operational sides. There were two large groups: partisans fighting in the mountains and other hard-to-reach areas, and those fighting in the cities against both Fascist and German troops.

The men behind the front in Italy; from the left Dr Rudolf Rahn, the Reich's plenipotentiary in Italy 1943–45, Field Marshal Rodolfo Graziani, Mussolini's commander of the Italian armed forces fighting on the German side, and Karl Wolff, the supreme SS and police commander in Italy. (Count Ernesto G. Vitetti)

They operated in small groups, mainly conducting sabotage actions against communication and transport lines in the north-west of Italy. From March 1944, AOK 10 hunted down partisan groups in its rear areas.

Partisan activity became a more serious concern for both Mussolini's Repubblica Sociale Italiana (RSI) and the Germans, who faced an increased threat shortly after the Allied landing at Anzio. One of the main partisan attacks against the German forces is related to this. In Rome on 23 March 1944 partisans planted a bomb that killed 33 policemen of the third battalion of the Polizei Regiment 'Bozen'. This unit was made up of members of the Ordnungspolizei (the uniformed police) recruited in the border region of South Tyrol, politically belonging to Italy, but with a large majority of ethnic Austrians. Some of them had served in the Italian armed forces, and enlisted in the newly formed Regiment 'Bozen' in 1943. They were not SS members, although the unit (along with every other unit of the Ordnungspolizei) was given the title 'SS-Polizei Regiment' in May 1944.

Hitler immediately demanded a large-scale reprisal and the next day the Sicherheitspolizei (the security police) killed 335 Italians, including a large number of Jews, and buried them in the Ardeatine Caves outside Rome. The figure included five extra hostages who had been taken as a precautionary measure and that were killed to avoid leaving witnesses behind. In post-war Italy the Ardeatine Cave massacre was upheld as an example of the brutality of the German occupation, but the facts are still far from clear.

The American writer Dr Richard Raiber has pointed out that historical research and analysis of this event is inadequate, if not completely absent. He questions whether Kesselring was even in Rome, believing that he was at La Spezia, where the US Rangers who took part in Operation *Ginny* were killed. After the war General Anton Dostler was tried and executed for this, while in Raiber's account, Kesselring and the other German generals committed perjury at their own trials.

The confusion surrounding the Ardeatine Caves killing provides an insight into the confusion that reigned in Italy after the Italian surrender. On 10 September 1943 Hitler installed civil and military commanders in Italy. SS-Obergruppenführer and General der Waffen-SS Karl Wolff, formerly chief of Heinrich Himmler's personal staff, was in charge of civil matters, while military command was given to the Army general Rudolf Toussaint, formerly attaché in Rome. This soon led to friction between the army and the SS in the matters of security; Hitler's orders of 12 September and 10 October gave authority in the operations area (including the coastal areas) to the operational commands, while the rear area fell within the competence of Toussaint. In December 1943 Kesselring's orders led to a fragmentation of the situation; given the lack of forces, competences on security matters fell into the hands of either the army or the SS, according to the local availability of commanders and forces. Wolff's organization, that included both security police and uniformed police, rapidly spread across the Italian territory, and SS and police officers took control of some army units, which caused even more resentments. On 23 January 1944, with Himmler's approval, Wolff established on his own initiative a local SS-und-Polizeiführer Oberitalien (SS and police command in northern Italy).

On 22 March 1944 Kesselring held a meeting with the Reich's ambassador to the RSI, Dr Rudolf Rahn, Richthofen, and Wolff, followed on the 30th by Kesselring's order that Wolff must cooperate with Toussaint and the army. On 3 April Himmler and Wolff declared that the non-operational parts of Italian territory were to be classified as *Bandenkampfgebiet* (anti-partisan combat territory), and two more SS-und-Polizeiführer were created, one in northern-central Italy (Oberitalien Mitte), another one in central Italy (Mittelitalien). Kesselring tried to regain control, but then suggested that Wolff take over control of the anti-partisan operations in Italy (outside operation areas). On 1 May OKW issued its own directive that sanctioned his proposal and on 10 May Kesselring issued a new order which put overall control of anti-partisan operations into his own hands. The anti-partisan war became a matter for Wolff and his men, at least outside the operation areas. In July Wolff reached the height of his power, when he replaced Toussaint as Bevollmächtigter General der Deutschen Wehrmacht in Italien. With Mussolini's RSI troops also active against the partisans, it is clear that the whole anti-partisan war in Italy was both fragmented and chaotic.

The post-war trials of German war criminals have been broken down by the German historian Kerstin von Lingen into three different phases; 1945–46 (basically the Nuremberg trials and some specific trials related to the killing of Allied soldiers and prisoners of war); 1946–48; and 1949–52, when the matter of the German rearmament changed the outlook. Trials against German war criminals were in most cases conducted by military courts of different states, rather than the International Military Tribunal. In 1947–48 the largest proceeding was held by a US Military Court at Nuremberg, the so-called 'High Command Trial', or 'United States of America vs. Wilhelm von Leeb, et al.' Fourteen German generals were on trial and at its conclusion in October 1948, two were sentenced to life terms, five others were sentenced to 15 to 20 years imprisonment, four received sentences of three to eight years, two were acquitted and one committed suicide while in custody. Most of the defendants were released either shortly after the trial ended or in 1954 at the latest. Hugo Sperrle, Kesselring's colleague in the 1940 air battles, was eventually acquitted from his charges and none of the high-level German field commanders (including Wilhelm von Leeb, Georg von Küchler, Hermann Hoth, Georg-Hans Reinhardt, Hans von Salmuth, Karl-Adolf Hollidt, Admiral Otto Schniewind, and Otto Wöhler) were sentenced to death.

The same did not apply to those who were put on trial by other nations such as the Soviet Union, Yugoslavia and Greece, for crimes committed in their territories. The 'Balkan Generals' case trial in February 1948 was an exception with eight generals sentenced to serve life imprisonment or from seven to 20 years. One (Maximilian von Weichs, Kesselring's equivalent in the Balkans) was withdrawn because of illness, and another one committed suicide. In almost every other case a death sentence was imposed. Twenty-one

Kesselring is escorted to the court during his trial in Venice by a British military policeman. (Private collection)

German generals were tried in the Soviet Union before late 1947, and most (15) were sentenced to death and executed, only six being sentenced to 25 years imprisonment (without early release). Yugoslavia tried 13 German generals, all of whom were sentenced to death and executed, and even Greece put three German generals on trial, with two of them sentenced to death and the third to life imprisonment.

British military courts pursued not only crimes committed against British soldiers and citizens, but also tried German officers responsible for committing war crimes in Italy against the Italians. Until 1949 a rough and incomplete count gives a total of 230 sentences to death, 447 to imprisonment and 260 acquitted from charges. British military courts tried and executed the only Italian war criminal to suffer such a fate, a man responsible for the killing of a British POW during an escape attempt.

From the beginning, the aim was ambitious. British courts intended to judge almost every high-level German commander that fought in Italy (and their chiefs of staff), including some field commanders directly involved in war crimes, and SS commanders such as Wolff; Harster, Himmler's representative in Italy; Eugen Dollmann; and Herbert Kappler, the SS commander in Rome directly responsible for the Ardeatine Caves killing. However, some of them eventually escaped trial thanks to their involvement in the surrender of the German forces in Italy (Operation *Sunrise*). Wolff, for example, was tried several times by British and German tribunals and was sentenced to imprisonment, without serving much of a sentence. Eventually, the Ardeatine Caves killing became a cause célèbre for the war crimes committed in Italy. On 18 October 1946 generals Eberhard von Mackensen (former commander of AOK 14) and Kurt Mälzer (former military commander of Rome) were tried in Rome for this particular episode, and both were sentenced to death on 30 November. Both had their sentence commuted to life imprisonment on 4 July 1947, along with Albert Kesselring.

Kesselring's trial, held separately, started in Venice on 17 February 1947, and was intended to set the standard for future trials of war criminals. Unsurprisingly, it ended on 6 May with a death sentence. Soon after, statements from several high-ranking personalities in the United Kingdom, including Churchill and Field Marshal Alexander, criticized the sentence, saying that Kesselring had been a brave soldier who fought with honour. On 4 July 1947 Kesselring had his sentence commuted to life imprisonment and in October was returned to Germany in British custody.

Between August and December 1949 other German generals were put under trial, although this time things took quite a different course and justice was tempered with mercy. Walther von Brauchitsch, Kesselring's equivalent in the West, died in October 1948; Generalfeldmarschall Gerd von Rundstedt was released on health grounds before the trial ended; and his colleague

Erich von Manstein was sentenced to 18 years, later reduced to 12 (he was also released on health grounds in May 1953). Subsequent trials of SS Major Walter Reder (unit commander in the 16. SS-Panzergrenadier Division), and of the Hermann Göring commander Wilhelm Schmalz, showed that the units committing war crimes were unaware of Kesselring's order of 21 August 1944 deploring incidents which 'damaged the German Wehrmacht's reputation and discipline and which no longer have anything to do with reprisal operations'.

By the early 1950s the wind had turned, and the debate about German rehabilitation had begun. On 8 July 1952 Kesselring (who had been working for the US Army Historical Division) underwent surgery for cancer, while veterans' associations restored his name. In the same year he was given honorary chairmanship of the Verband Deutsches Afrika-Korps (the Afrika Korps veterans' association) and of the Stahlhelm, the 'steel helmet' association. Eventually, Kesselring was released on 23 October 1952 (in the same year Mälzer died in prison, while Mackensen was released too), holding a press conference two days later. In 1953 he published his memoirs, partly based on the work he did for the Historical Division, *Soldat bis zum letzten Tag* (*Soldier to the last day*, published in English simply as *Memoirs*), followed in 1955 by the second part, *Gedanken zum Zweiten Weltkrieg* (*Thoughts on World War II*). Five years later he did not fade away, like other old soldiers, but simply died.

A LIFE IN WORDS

When dealing with the life and history of Albert Kesselring one faces several different perspectives. Biographers either provide a vision of a remarkable officer and commander who won the respect and admiration of his own soldiers and of his enemies alike, or an alternate view of the classic 'Prussian' style general, directly responsible for some of the most atrocious war crimes committed during World War II. Studies of Kesselring's activity as a soldier are usually fragmentary, and often discordant. He was directly responsible for the cancellation of the plans for the German strategic bomber, or possibly (as we have seen) simply carrying out Wever's plans. He was a brilliant leader of Luftflotte 1 and 2 during the most spectacular years of the German blitzkrieg, winning the air wars against Poland, Holland and Belgium, and France. But he was also behind the eventual failures of Dunkirk and the Battle of Britain, although this is usually regarded as the achievement of the RAF against an overwhelming enemy, rather than Kesselring's, and Germany's, own failure. The role he played in the first phases of Operation *Barbarossa* is barely mentioned, although some of his most interesting remarks (and possibly later successes) were formed by his experiences in the Soviet Union.

The war in the Mediterranean saw Kesselring at the peak of his career. Almost every account, covering either his life or Rommel's, emphasizes the differences and rivalry between the two generals, and the effect this had on the eventual outcome of the battles fought in North Africa and in the Mediterranean. The Malta or Tobruk issue represents a basic strategic decision that became a cornerstone of the war, and most commentators now accept Kesselring's view that the seizure of Malta would have maintained the flow of supplies to North Africa, eventually sparing Rommel the failure at El Alamein. Kesselring's liaison role between Hitler, the OKW and the Italians deserves closer scrutiny, because it was critically important.

The Italian campaign is Kesselring's real trademark, even though it was the end of his career. The campaign fought from Salerno to Rome brought disillusionment, disappointments, failures and frustrations to the Allies, who came to regard their opponents with a bitter and grudging respect. Many Allied failures can be explained – Salerno was chosen as a landing area because it was considered safer than Rome, in spite of the prize the latter was to offer, and the German counterattacks came as a real shock to the Allied forces. Even more shocking was the fact that the conduct of war seemed to move back in time and reverted to the style of World War I. The bitter, step-by-step advance across a land that seemed to offer nothing else than one more hill, one more river and one more mountain was hard and both the soldiers and the people at home justified it by explaining that the enemy they were fighting was the best in the world, and their commanders outstanding. And this may explain how Kesselring eventually became a 'master strategist', to use the words of his biographer. All too often it is easier to glorify your enemy rather than blame your own leaders.

In this respect Anzio is an interesting case. The commander of the US VI Corps is generally blamed for his failure to exploit the tactical advantage of surprise, which allowed the German defences to remain entrenched. But it is worth noting that Kesselring was well-prepared for a surprise landing and had a plan in place to contain the enemy, if not one to counterattack and wipe out the beachhead. This is the crux of the Kesselring problem: all too often there is a very thin line separating his own successes from his enemies' failures, and which gives a distorted image of his career. The view of Kesselring as a good commander shifts to a more critical picture, which enhances his weaknesses and deficiencies.

For example, the Luftwaffe victories in 1939–41 were the result of both its own strengths and of its enemies' weaknesses, in particular when the air battles were fought at Dunkirk and over the skies of Britain. The seizure of Malta could have the supply problems in the Mediterranean, but had Rommel been able to seize Alexandria, an even better solution would have been available.

The lack of detailed studies, in particular with regard to the Luftwaffe's blitzkrieg years and to the German view of the Italian campaign, has contributed to the contrasting views of Kesselring's life and career as a soldier, a commander and a strategist. It is really a matter of perspective. As Kesselring said, he was a soldier to the last day, but he fought a vicious war with vicious measures that led to events that can hardly be justified, and sometimes only just understood.

BIBLIOGRAPHY AND
FURTHER READING

Albert Kesselring's own memoirs, the 1953 *Soldat bis zum letzten Tag* and 1955 *Gedanken zum Zweiten Weltkrieg*, are an excellent starting point.

Kenneth Macksey's *Kesselring: The Making of the Luftwaffe*, alternatively available as *Kesselring: German Master Strategist of World War II* (first published 1978, reprint with the alternate title 1996), provides a valuable portrait, although it lacks a little analytical depth. Most recent books dealing with Kesselring are devoted to his trial and only offer brief biographical portraits without details. They are excellent works, nevertheless: Kerstin von Lingen's *Kesselrings letzte Schlacht* (2004, published in English as *Kesselring's last battle*), and Richard Raiber's *Anatomy of a Perjury: Field Marshal Albert Kesselring, via Rasella, and the Ginny Mission* (2008) are exhaustive and detailed, although for a more complete view one should also read Michael Salter's *Nazi War Crimes, US Intelligence and Selective Prosecution at Nuremberg* (2007).

There are many books about the Luftwaffe during World War II, and a good starting point is Williamson Murray's *Luftwaffe – Strategy for Defeat 1933–45*. James Corum's *The Luftwaffe: Creating the Operational Air War, 1918–1940* (1997) and *Wolfram von Richthofen: Master of the German Air War* (2008) are valuable additions. Horst Boog's *Die Deutsche Luftwaffenführung 1935–1945* (1982) is essential to understand Luftwaffe generalship and command. There are no German accounts of the early air war in 1939–41, particularly about the campaign in the West and the Battle of Britain, although the latter is covered in Udo Volkmann's *Die Britische Luftverteidigung* (1982). The US Air Force Historical Research Agency's German historical studies do cover the period and offer interesting insights, but should be read with hindsight.

For the Mediterranean, there are two books that ought not to be missed: Karl Gundelach's *Die deutsche Luftwaffe im Mittelmeer 1940–1945* (two volumes, 1981), and Ralf Georg Reuth's *Entscheidung im Mittelmeer* (1985). A list of books or articles dealing with the Italian campaign would probably take more space than this volume, although those actually dealing with the German side (and using German sources) are very scarce. There are four German studies worth mentioning. Josef Schröder's *Italiens Kriegsaustritt 1943* (1969); Jörg Steiger's *Anzio – Nettuno. Eine Schlacht der Führungsfehler* (1962); Katriel Ben Arie's *Die Schlacht bei Monte Cassino 1944* (1986); and Karl-Heinz Golla's *Zwischen Reggio und Cassino* (2004). The works of Gerhard Schreiber, Germany's leading expert on Italy and World War II, should also be read, especially with regard to the German war crimes; see in particular his *Deutsche Kriegsverbrechen in Italien* (1996).

INDEX